Also by Margaret Boyles

The Margaret Boyles Book of Needle Art
Needlepoint Stitchery
Bargello: An Explosion in Color
American Indian Needlepoint Workbook
The Margaret Boyles Bargello Workbook

The Margaret Boyles Book of
CREWEL EMBROIDERY

SIMON AND SCHUSTER   NEW YORK

All photography by the author. Assistance with black and white photography by Margaret Hope Boyles.

Published by Simon and Schuster
A Division of Gulf & Western Corporation
Simon & Schuster Building
Rockefeller Center
1230 Avenue of the Americas
New York, New York 10020

Designed by Jill Weber

Manufactured in the United States of America

1 2 3 4 5 6 7 8 9 10

Library of Congress Cataloging in Publication Data

Boyles, Margaret.
   The Margaret Boyles book of crewel
embroidery.

   1. Crewelwork. I. Title. II. Title:
Book of crewel embroidery.
TT778.C7B68   746.4'4   79-13430
ISBN 0-671-24616-X

Acknowledgment

My gratitude and thanks to my daughter, Margaret Hope, who contributed her knowledge and spent long hours in the darkroom with me, perfecting the black and white photographs. Her help and assistance were invaluable in the last days of hectic production.

Dedication

This book is dedicated with great affection to my dear friend, Constance Schrader, who "found" me at Macy's and has advanced my career with unselfish advice, assistance, wisdom, and love through the years of our association. There is none other like her!

Contents

A Note from the Author

In response to many requests for my crewel designs and instructions, I have put together this collection, which I hope pleases the loyal readers who asked for it. You will find my favorite designs that lean toward the historical and traditional, a few Oriental themes, some modern florals, and some childlike illustrations for the ABCs. Colors, the Boyles hallmark, range from delicate to bright, sometimes monochromatic, sometimes polychromatic, sometimes softly traditional as in the colonial embroideries, but always "Boyles."

Knowledge of the romance and history surrounding an embroidery enhances my enjoyment of it, and I hope to share that knowledge with you in a short survey touching on the high points of the history of embroidery with wool.

As is my practice, I have tried to put together a collection of designs that will appeal to a wide range of tastes, but I must admit that they are all inescapably mine. As usual, with each design I have included complete instructions and material requirements so every one can be duplicated exactly. The Stitch Dictionary shows the mechanics of many stitches photographically, in a manner that makes learning a new stitch easy even for a beginner. A short chapter introduces the beginner to crewel embroidery and suggests three projects planned to teach a good working vocabulary of stitches. Working hints in another chapter lead both the beginner and the more experienced into embroidery and answer the most frequently asked questions about techniques. Finally, blocking, mounting, and finishing are discussed, and instructions are included so every project can be entirely yours from the very first stitch to the last nail in the frame or tassel on a pillow.

It adds up to a complete book on crewel embroidery with enough designs and suggestions to keep you busy and happy for a long time. I hope you will enjoy this experience with me and will learn and grow and begin to create your own designs—your part of crewel's history to be passed on to future generations.

Sincerely, *Margaret Boyles*

THE HANCOCK COVERLET, 1725–1750, New England.

Introduction

Knowledge of the origins of crewel embroidery has disintegrated along with the yarns and fabrics of the first pieces, leaving us to speculate about those early articles and those who made them. Some evidences of wool embroidery suggest that it was known to the Greeks and Romans: a fragment of cloth excavated in Northern Mongolia bearing the face of a nomad warrior is attributed to the first century before Christ; a few obscure biblical references suggest that curtains, altar cloths, or other hangings embellished with wool embroidery may have decorated early Jewish tabernacles.

Although this evidence points to the use of wool for embroidery for centuries, the word "crewel" referred to the wool yarn, not to the type of embroidery. Crewels (sometimes cruells) were two-ply, tightly twisted wool yarns used for both canvas work and embroidery. Thus, any embroidery worked with these yarns could properly be called crewel. Not until recent years was the term "crewel embroidery" applied specifically to the type of embroidery with which this book deals.

Because much of the old embroidery has vanished and little has been recorded to establish the facts of its history, it is difficult to write a concise chronicle of its development. A few surviving old pieces plus occasional references in wills, diaries, inventories, and other writings give us some insight into how the embroidery was used and the esteem in which it was held.

Perhaps the most important of the surviving ancient wool embroideries is the Bayeux Tapestry, a truly remarkable piece approximately 230 feet long by 20 inches wide, depicting in

---

Now in the possession of the Winterthur Museum, this lovely linen coverlet, embroidered entirely with wool, was originally owned by Thomas Hancock, a wealthy Boston merchant, and may have been made for him at the time of his marriage in 1730. Upon Thomas's death, it was inherited by John Hancock, signer of the Declaration of Independence, and can be traced directly through the family to its present place in the museum.

Like many coverlets of its day, its embroidery features oak and pine trees, scroll-shaped vines, and exotic birds. The polychrome design is worked in Flat, Outline, Satin, Buttonhole, and Seed Stitches.

COURTESY, THE HENRY FRANCIS DU PONT
WINTERTHUR MUSEUM.

1

seventy-two animated sequences the Norman conquest of England in 1066. Although misnamed—it is not a tapestry but crewel embroidery—this miraculously preserved piece is a delightful pictorial narrative full of historical detail worked in eight colors of crewel yarn on a bleached linen background. The stitches used include Outline, Couching, and Laid Work (a form of Couching). Presumably the piece was worked by a group of embroiderers, but this detail and the exact date the work was completed cannot be positively established, although it is assumed that the work was done in the period immediately following the Battle of Hastings.

The embroidery is now on view in a gallery in an old chateau near the Church of Notre Dame in Bayeux. On visiting the exhibit, one is impressed by the great length of the "tapestry" (77 yards), the careful draftsmanship, the detail

of the narrative, and other technical aspects, but overriding all is a sense of wonder that in times so long past, the needle, stitches, and color were all used much as we use them today. The piece is an emotional and artistic link with the past for embroiderers as well as for students of history.

We know that the art of embroidery was practiced during the Middle Ages. Knowledge and manufacture of the modern needle reached Nuremberg in the last quarter of the fourteenth century and spread through Europe reaching England, where it was first manufactured in 1545. Shortly thereafter, Elizabeth I became queen, and we find evidence of a great deal of beautiful embroidery. Elizabethans enjoyed an increasing prosperity—they loved the theater, fancy clothes, jewelry, sports, dancing, music, and books. The middle class expanded, homes began to change, and carpets, cushions, hangings, and other furnishings were needed to warm them and make them more comfortable. It was natural for the more affluent to use embroidery as adornment wherever practical. Most of this embroidery was in silk on silk, linen, wool, or linen canvas. Very little was worked entirely with wool—there was still no crewel embroidery as we know it today.

During the reign of James I (the first quarter of the seventeenth century), the name "Jacobean" came into use, and it was shortly after this time that the exotic designs most often associated with crewel embroidery were developed and refined. Presumably, this was the re-

POCKET, 1750–1800, American.
Embroidered in three shades of blue with accents of gold and beige, this pocket was fashioned to be tied around the waist to hold all manner of necessities. Made of plain linen and worked in Roumanian Couching, Outline, Chain, and Ladder Stitches, this one is particularly lovely.

COURTESY, THE HENRY FRANCIS DU PONT WINTERTHUR MUSEUM.

VALANCE, 1740–1760, New England.

In the eighteenth century the master bed was often the most important piece of furniture in the home, and it was usually furnished with elaborate hangings for the dual purpose of decoration and protection from the cold. Embroidered hangings were relatively uncommon, but a few have survived. A complete set would include three valances, which hung from the tester, a headcloth, four curtains, a coverlet, and, occasionally, three bases which attached to the side and end rails of the bed and hung to the floor.

This lovely valance survives as an example of the graceful design, stitching, and coloring preferred at that time in New England.

COURTESY, MUSEUM OF FINE ARTS, BOSTON.

sult of increased trade mainly by the East India Company that imported to England painted cottons from India. These imports introduced many of the favorite crewel design elements—the tree of life, hillocks, imaginative flowers, huge exotic leaves, small frolicking animals. At this time it became common practice to work entirely with wool, and the influence of the embroidery worked during this period was felt for many years later.

About the same time, the settlement of the colonies began, and embroidery was carried across the ocean. In the beginning, there was not time for leisurely pursuit of the art, but as soon as the early settlers had built and furnished their first homes, the natural instinct to beautify their surroundings exerted itself, and we find the most affluent of the settlers placing orders for crewels and fabrics from London.

Those who could afford it ordered dimity and fustian and colored yarns from London. Others began weaving their own linens, spinning and dyeing yarns. Recipes for natural dyes were exchanged, and virtually every home had its own indigo pot in which yarn was steeped to attain various shades of blue. Sumac, madder, goldenrod, sheep laurel, cochineal, and logwood were among the other materials used to complete a lovely palette.

Memories of England kept the Jacobean designs in the forefront as inspiration for the early colonial pieces, but gradually native American flowers and animals replaced the English originals, and a scarcity of materials necessitated opening up the design to expose more background fabric. It is conjectured that the expense of yarns was responsible for the popularity of some of the stitches that became the hallmark of colonial embroideries, for most of them used less yarn as compared to many of the English favorites. A new style of crewel—simpler, more elegant, and truly American—emerged. This remained in vogue through the seventeenth and eighteenth centuries and was used lavishly on bed hangings, coverlets, cushions, petticoats, tablecloths, fire screens, pictures, aprons, pocketbooks, dresses, and waistcoats.

Gradually, as styles in dress, furniture, and home decoration changed, the use of crewel faded. Fortunately, some of the best pieces were packed away and now grace our museums. In 1898 there was a short-lived revival of crewel in Deerfield, Massachusetts, by the Blue and White Society, which meticulously copied old local pieces, working them in either linen or wool threads in shades of blue. The revival was important economically to the town, but interest gradually faded and the society was disbanded. Museums in Deerfield own a treasure of these lovely pieces, as well as many of the drawings and notebooks of the embroiderers and founders of the society.

As the twentieth century dawned, there was little crewel being made; a whole generation of embroiderers grew up not knowing the word or the work. About mid-century, interest in the historic restoration of several towns spawned an inquiry into the embroideries and folk arts of the colonial period. A few excellent books explored crewel embroidery, and there were a few scattered classes taught mostly by women who had known and worked with crewel for many years in the museums. Gradually interest grew until suddenly there was a great revival of the art. Manufacturers began to sell kits containing yarn and fabric with designs already stamped, ready for embroidery; many more books were written; magazines carried articles and instructions, TV offered mini-courses; every craft center had an instructor and classes in the art; everywhere there were people working away at their embroidery and finding it was fun! Crewel was back and enjoying a success as great or greater than ever before in its long history.

It is interesting to survey the crewel kits and pattern designs available today for they run the gamut from exact duplication of historic pieces to designs in the most modern manner. Stitches and color have really changed very little for we have researched the stitches documenting those used and found them still to be the best. We have also found that the original colors of most of the historic pieces were as bright and vigorous as the ones we ourselves love. Time and oxidation have, in most cases, softened the once lively colors to their present shades.

An interesting outgrowth of the current revival of crewel has been the development of "creative stitchery" which is really a free adaptation of the embroidery, using many of the original stitches and a variety of different yarns to "paint" pictures. Generally the stitches are large and the yarn heavy but carefully used for special effects: white angora may make a dandelion head ready to be blown away by the wind, Turkey Work loops of yellow knitting worsted suggest summer's zinnia, Straight Stitches in long lengths can be flower stems or shading; imagination has free reign and the effect is wonderful.

There are the purists who disdain creative stitchery, pointing out that traditional crewel is

BRADSTREET CHAIR SEATS, 1725–1750, New England.

4

always worked within a discipline that produces exquisite stitches and uses them only in certain prescribed manners on very special fabrics, but unfortunately these embroiderers have lost sight of the fact that if our forebears had not indulged their own creativity, we would still be covering entire fabrics with Tudor and Jacobean patterns, and whole centuries of innovative design would have been omitted. It is undeniably true that much modern embroidery is bad—poorly designed, improperly worked with little attention to craftsmanship, embroidered on cheap or inappropriate fabric with poor yarn—but it is also true that a great deal of truly excellent work is being produced. Some of the embroidery currently being done—even some from commercial kits—is of a quality to rival some of the most revered museum examples.

The important thing for the modern embroiderer to do is to master the craft, learn all the basics, then adventure with the needle and yarn to produce truly original embroideries that are a reflection of life in the last quarter of the twentieth century and a mirror of the embroiderer's own personality. We should improvise on a firm foundation of skills, picture life with its joys and hopes, and always remember that the beautiful old museum treasures were made by people much like ourselves, urged on by an inner drive to create beauty but never dreaming that centuries later their work would be studied and copied. Only thus will we pass on to succeeding generations something of ourselves. It is not outrageous to conjecture that some of the best—maybe even some of the junk—will find its way into the museums of tomorrow. In this way the legacy of the past—the long history, the stitches, the designs and techniques of crewel embroidery—becomes part of our bequest to future generations.

There is great joy and serene pleasure in crewel embroidery. Spend a quiet hour shading a green leaf, a happy time embroidering one of Mary Breed's amusing little birds, a cheerful interval working a sunny bouquet of flowers, or a few moments working out the intricacies of a new stitch, and in this way come to appreciate the reasons this embroidery has endured and

Whimsically designed and worked predominantly in Flat Stitch, these four chair seats are from a prominent Boston Puritan family. The designs are typical of the period, featuring solidly worked hillocks in the foreground and the imaginative birds, deer, pine trees, and stylized flowers.

COURTESY, MUSEUM OF FINE ARTS, BOSTON.

been loved for so long. Learn to appreciate crewel embroidery for the richness it can add to leisure time, the pleasure of its beauty in the home, for there is something intangible in the appeal of this old needle art—something in the gleam in the embroidered eye of that first century warrior, something in the stance of the horses and the majesty of the ships on the Bayeux Tapestry, something in the innocent charm of Mary Breed's bird-inhabited trees—something elusive in woolen stitches that enchants and captures the imagination.

THE MARY BREED BEDSPREAD, 1770, New England.

Nothing is known about the Breed family except that the family home was on Breed's hill near Bunker Hill in Boston. Mary's coverlet may have originally been two narrow curtains and three valances. The design is notable for its rigidly symmetrical trees, whimsical birds, and scattered floral motifs. The embroidery, which is polychrome and predominately Flat Stitch on linen, is signed by Mary Breed and dated 1770.

COURTESY, THE METROPOLITAN MUSEUM OF ART.

THE MATERIALS FOR CREWEL EMBROIDERY

Yarns

The word "crewel" is derived from an old Welsh word that means wool. Colonial crewels were two-ply, lightly twisted wool yarns. Therefore, embroidery worked with a wool thread is crewel, and only that embroidery can be properly classified as true crewel.

Colonial American crewel was worked in hand-spun, vegetable-dyed wool or crewels as they were called. These were lovely, precious, and carefully used in stitches that wasted as little yarn as possible. The colors had that intangible beauty produced only with vegetable dyes.

Although it is much easier to use the lovely yarns on the market today, it is possible to re-create the Colonial yarns and colors. The revival of interest in old crafts has brought about renewed research into methods and processes of natural dyeing which are being taught at craft centers and workshops across the country. Weavers are particularly interested in spinning and dyeing by the traditional methods, and though they are likely to be working with heavier yarns than those used for crewel, their meth-

ods would apply to crewel yarns as well, making a weaving center a good place to start looking if you are interested in dyeing your own yarns. Also check the library and bookstore for several of the recently published, very good handbooks on natural dyeing.

The three-ply, Persian-type yarns currently available are perfect for most crewel embroidery. They are generally of good quality and come in a dazzling array of colors. Most can be purchased in either 10- or 25-yard skeins, while others can be obtained in 1-yard strands. These yarns work very well: make lovely soft stitches, do not wear thin if the proper length is used, are generally fade resistant, and many are moth-proofed. Colors range from bright contemporary hues to the softest of pastels, and a series of five or six shades to a color family is common, making shading a pleasure. The three-ply strand is convenient as the yarn can be used as is for very heavy work or separated to be used for finer stitches.

The beautiful, fine, single-ply British crewel wools are a joy to use. Their colors and texture are very special, so naturally the finished embroidery is lovely. Because the yarn is slightly finer and more expensive than domestic yarns, many teachers feel these British yarns should be used by more experienced embroiderers. Working with them is slightly different than with our yarns, but it is definitely a rewarding experience, and many people can never go back to other yarns once they have used the British crewels.

Increasingly, synthetic yarns are coming into the picture, and many look and perform enough like wool to be satisfactory substitutes. Many of the past problems with these synthetics have been eliminated: some lacked the soft resilience of wool; others wore thin when used; still others could not duplicate the soft luster of wool or the pleasant working qualities. We will soon see crewels of synthetics that combine all the good qualities of both the natural and the synthetic fibers.

The majority of projects in this book have been worked with my favorite Columbia-Minerva Needlepoint and Crewel Yarn, and the color numbers that appear in the instructions are for that yarn. It is available in both 10- and 25-yard skeins in an enticing array of colors.

The color numbers in the instructions also apply to Paternayan Crewel Yarn. The two yarns can be used interchangeably as both are wool, and color numbers and standards are the same. Occasionally a color number appears with an asterisk (*) after it. This indicates that the particular color is available only in the Paternayan range.

To make the substitution of other yarns possible, yarn quantities for each project are given in yards rather than in skeins. The quantities apply to three-ply strands regardless of the number of strands with which the stitches are worked.

The quantities of yarn listed for each project should be adequate for the average careful worker to finish each piece with a small surplus. The working methods used to determine the estimates were normal ones with no special emphasis on conservation of yarn, but no material was wasted. If you know you are extravagant with yarn or decide to change stitches, buy a little extra just to be sure you do not run short.

Although crewel is technically only embroidery worked with wool, the designs in this book are suitable for other materials, and for the sake of illustration, some are shown in other threads. In some of the very tiny designs, cotton embroidery floss is obviously a better choice than wool, and for reasons of practicality, clothing that is going to need washing is better worked with cotton. There are also other threads that will adapt well to most of the designs: linen, many imported cottons of various weights, silk, and the synthetics. Feel free to experiment; you will probably prefer the springy wool for its texture and general appearance, but it is good to know the other materials are available.

Fabrics

Colonial crewel embroidery was worked on a variety of grades and weaves of linen fabric, some of which were domestic and handwoven while others were imported from England. In the seventeenth and eighteenth centuries, most families raised flax, harvested, and prepared it for spinning and weaving. The availability of the linen as well as its excellent wearing qualities established it as a favorite material for embroidery. The natural or slightly bleached colors provided a perfect background for the lovely home-dyed crewel yarn colors and the combination remains unsurpassed.

Although the names cambric and lawn are now associated with cotton fabric, in Colonial times these were made of linen and were among the prized imports used for embroidery. Dimity, an all-cotton ribbed fabric, was occasionally used as was fustian. The latter was a twill, woven with a linen warp and cotton weft. It was used extensively in England, less frequently in America.

By comparison, the variety of fabrics available today would astonish our ancestors. Excellent European linens, in many weights and weaves, compete with lovely domestics, while cottons, wools, and some new synthetics provide additional variety. There is so much that finding the proper fabric for each project is easy.

Choose fabric for embroidery keeping in mind the overall effect desired and the final use of the piece, as well as the cost. For upholstery only the best quality heavy linen should be used; for slip seats and stool tops, which are easy to replace, a slightly lighter fabric can be chosen, but it should still be one that resists abrasion and will maintain its good looks for a long time; pictures and decorative pillows may be worked on a finer, softer fabric.

Recently, excellent quality, colored linen has begun to make an appearance. This adds much to the possibilities for pillows, fashion accessories, and pictures when a colored background is required. Some of the good dress linens can also be used for items that will not be subjected to very hard wear. The myriad of colors in which they are produced makes them especially desirable.

Some muslins and cottons with a hand-spun look are appropriate for crewel embroidery. Luxurious soft afghans can be made from wool or wool and synthetic blends with a firm weave and smooth surface. Good wool serge is hard to find in appropriate colors but, when available, is a good background for wool embroidery.

The beginner should choose a smooth finish, tightly woven linen or high-thread-count cotton or muslin for a first project. Crewel is easiest to work on a tightly woven fabric. Homespun and other rough textures make it difficult to produce even stitches, and the background competes with the embroidery. Avoid loosely woven fabrics which stretch and are very difficult to use.

Good quality is essential as embroidery, like other needle arts, is easier with good materials. When purchasing material for a project, keep in mind the many hours that will go into the project. You will agree that it is a shame to lavish that much time, talent, and yarn on an unworthy fabric.

Needles

The crewel needle is fairly thick with a sharp point and long tapered eye. It is made in various sizes to accommodate different weights of yarn. Ideally the needle should pierce the fabric easily, making an opening just large enough for the yarn to pass through without too much friction.

Find the best quality needles available as less expensive ones corrode quickly and are difficult to use. Keep a selection of sizes on hand and experiment to find the best for you and your project.

Thimbles

Use a thimble if you are in the habit of using it for other sewing, but do not fret if you find it is more trouble than it is worth. Beautiful embroidery can be worked with or without a thimble, and it is purely a matter of personal preference.

Scissors

Good embroidery scissors are a must, and they should be used for embroidery only. Find a small 3-inch to 4-inch pair with blades that are sharp to the very tips, and keep them in a case to protect both them and your embroidery.

Transfer Pencils

Transfer or copy pencils make the job of putting the designs on fabric an easy one-step task. Available in most needlework shops at very nominal cost, these are made in magenta, yellow, and blue.

They replace dressmaker carbon, pouncing, and all the other old methods for transferring patterns to fabric. If you use the pencil to trace the design from the book, the tracing is ready to be used as a transfer pattern with no additional work needed. Lines created with this type of transfer are fairly permanent and will not rub off when the piece is embroidered. Some wash out more easily than others, but those that do not come off with soap and water can usually be removed with cleaning fluid.

Tracing Paper

Since you will be tracing the designs and using the same tracing for the transfer pattern, it is best to use a fairly heavy paper like that found in pads in art supply stores. Most of these will stand up to the heat of the iron and provide enough protection to the fabric to prevent scorching.

Hoops and Frames

It is best to work crewel with the fabric stretched taut in a hoop or frame. This requires a little adjustment in learning to work with one hand above and one hand under the work, but with a little practice, this becomes automatic, and the stitching is very fast, stitches are beautiful, and there is never any bunching from too tight tension.

The picture shows several styles of hoops: hand-held, freestanding, and roller type. All are satisfactory and choice should be made according to the project at hand and your personal preference.

The round freestanding style is probably the best all-around choice. It has a screw-type fastener that makes it possible to stretch the fabric very tightly and to keep it that way. The stand leaves both hands free, the hoop itself swivels, and the height is adjustable to make working comfortable. The area of exposed work surface is about that of a 10-inch circle, which is adequate and means the hoop does not have to be moved too often.

The roller frame can be used with or without a floor stand. Many people prefer to use it propped against a table or chair arm, while others prefer one of the little "sit upon" stands or the larger floor stand. The advantages of this frame are that it accommodates large projects easily, adjusts to keep the fabric taut, and offers a large work surface. Extra side pieces in different lengths also make this frame even more versatile as it will fit a wide range of sizes.

Hand-held hoops in round and oval shapes come in many sizes. Look for wood or plastic with the little screw device to tighten and hold the fabric secure. Metal hoops may stain the fabric and so should generally be avoided.

The artist's stretcher frame is an inexpensive substitute for a hoop and is especially handy for large projects. The frame can be purchased to the exact size of the piece, and the entire design can be worked without moving the fabric. This is good when the stitches are long or loose and could be stretched out of shape by the rings of a hoop.

THE BASICS
OF
GOOD EMBROIDERY

To make it possible for you to duplicate exactly the projects shown in this book, each has been presented as a finished, photographed model, a full-size drawing with stitch and color notations, a complete list of materials needed, and detailed working instructions. You may duplicate exactly or change colors, fabric, even stitches. In effect, it is possible for you to assemble your own custom kit.

Fabric Requirements

Before purchasing supplies, read all the pages with information about the fabrics, yarns, and other materials used for the particular projects pictured. The list with each project details the minimum quantities required. Note that fabric dimensions are usually noted in exact size rather than in approximate yards. These measurements allow for borders and seam allowances and are supplied to make it possible for you to use small pieces of fabric that may be already on hand. If the piece is very small (as some of the pincushions), it may be necessary

to sew on side and end extensions of muslin or scrap fabric in order to put the piece in a frame or hoop. To do this, just add an extension to each of the four sides, sewing it firmly on the machine. When the embroidery is finished, cut the extensions off and discard. This procedure saves a great deal of fabric needed for many projects.

Yarn Requirements

Since crewel yarn is available in skeins of varying yardages, yarn requirements have been noted in yards rather than in skeins. These estimates have been based on three-ply strands. The color numbers are for Columbia-Minerva Needlepoint and Crewel Yarn unless otherwise stated. (See following section, Identification of Yarns and Stitches on the Charts.) Naturally, other brands of yarn may be substituted, but careful attention should be paid to yardage required.

The yardage suggested for each project is based on that used to finish the model shown.

There is variation in the ways people work—some tend to work loosely, some are very careful and sparing, while others apply yarn heavily—but this has been taken into consideration. The yardage specified should be sufficient for the average careful worker to complete the piece. If you know you are extravagant with yarn or if you intend to change stitches, you may want to buy extra to avoid running short in the middle of the work.

Identification of Yarns and Stitches on the Charts

Capital letters (A, B, etc.) on each chart indicate the stitches that were used on the model, while numbers identify the yarn or thread colors. The color numbers are the manufacturer's identifying numbers, and the names have been included to help with identification and substitution. Most of the crewel yarn numbers are for Columbia-Minerva Needlepoint and Crewel Yarn or the equally well-known Paternayan Crewel Yarn. In a few cases, the color is available only in Paternayan, and this is noted by an asterisk (*) after the color number. The two yarns can be mixed with no problem, as both are fine quality wool and use the same color standards.

Transferring Designs to Fabric

Line drawings of the exact size of the embroideries are provided for every project, so there will be no enlarging problems for those who cannot draw. Trace them with one of the new hot-iron or copy pencils and transfer them from the tissue without recopying. Note that the designs appear in this book in reverse position so that when transferred directly in the manner described, the pattern will be exactly like the finished model.

To join the sections of large designs that have been divided across two or more pages, trace them onto parchment that has been folded into half or quarters as directed, matching the fold lines on the paper to the dashed lines on the charts. When tracing adjoining sections, match up the overlapping portions of the drawings to insure proper alignment of the design sections. When the design has been divided thus, it is usually best to trace all parts first with an ordinary pencil, check to see that all sections match, then go over the drawing with the transfer pencil in preparation for ironing the design onto the fabric.

When tracing for the transfer, work with a very sharp pencil to keep the lines fine as they spread with the heat of the iron. If a mistake is made, begin over with a new sheet of paper since the error will transfer to the fabric and may be in an area that will not be covered with embroidery. Move the iron over the transfer pattern carefully to avoid displacing it or smearing the lines. It is best to make a small practice tracing and transfer it to the corner of the fabric to check iron temperature as well as visibility of the color pencil on the fabric. If a fairly heavy quality parchment or vellum paper is used, the heat of the iron should not scorch the fabric. If the fabric being used is delicate or the test transfer indicates a danger of scorching, add an extra layer of paper over the transfer pattern to protect the fabric.

The embroidery stitches should be worked to cover completely the transfer lines, but if, when the work is finished, some traces of lines are visible, washing with mild soap will remove most of them. Make a test sample and try washing. If this is not successful with that particular pencil, try cleaning fluid, then wash thoroughly to remove all traces of odor.

Sorting Yarns

Sort yarns in daylight and mark them with the color numbers to correspond to the ones on the charts. There are many ways to do this, and you will undoubtedly develop your own system. If you use either a plastic yarn palette or one of the slotted ruler-type sorters, you can mark the color numbers on the plastic with India ink which can be removed and changed for a new project. A similar arrangement can be made from a strip of cardboard with slots for yarn cut along one edge and numbers written in alongside the cuts. Although not as convenient, the yarn can be tied in skeins with tags attached for color numbers.

If the yarn is cut into working-length strands before it is attached to the sorter, it will save time when the embroidery is being worked.

Threading the Needle

Never wet or twist the yarn to thread the needle. Use one of the methods shown on the accompanying charts or use one of the small metal needle threaders.

Shown in the accompanying drawings are two methods of threading a needle with yarn. There is another simple but seldom described method that is entirely correct. Press the end of the yarn tightly between the thumb and forefinger of one hand. With the other hand, force the eye of the needle over the tightly held yarn. The yarn will fit right into the eye of the needle after only a little practice.

The paper method is always successful, even with yarn that tends to split or fray. Any of the three techniques is good.

FOLD METHOD

1. Hold the needle between the thumb and forefinger with the eye facing you. Fold the yarn across the needle and pull tightly to form a sharp fold. Hold the fold tightly and gently withdraw the needle.

2. Force the fold through the eye of the needle.

PAPER METHOD

1. Cut a small piece of paper about an inch long and narrow enough to fit through the eye of the needle. Fold the paper as shown in the drawing and place the cut end of the yarn in the fold.

2. Pass the folded end of the paper through the eye of the needle, and the yarn will be carried through easily.

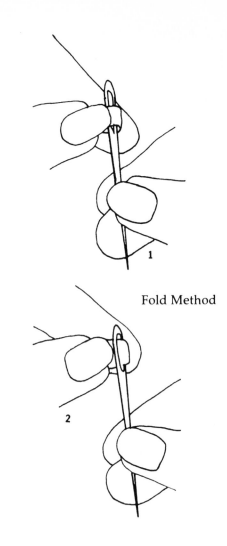

Fold Method

THREADING THE NEEDLE

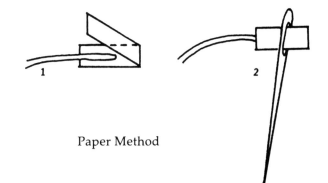

Paper Method

Stretching the Fabric in a Hoop or Frame

Crewel embroidery is much easier and the stitches faster and more even when the background fabric is stretched tightly into a hoop or frame. I like mine to be tight as a drum, but you may prefer a little less tension. This is a personal choice that can be made only after experimentation. Do, however, tighten the fabric enough to prevent any bunching or drawing up from tension on the stitches.

If a round hoop with a screw adjustment is to be used, tighten the screw so the two loops fit snugly without the fabric. Slip the top loop off. Spread the fabric over the lower section, centering the portion to be worked. Fit the top hoop over the fabric, working it down just enough to anchor it. Now gently tighten the fabric by pulling the edges. Push the hoop the rest of the way down.

Most round hoops have a working area that is smaller than that to be embroidered, meaning that the piece will have to be moved one or more times to be completed. Most crewel stitches are firm enough not to be damaged or stretched if the hoop is fastened on them, but the hoop should always be removed when the embroidery is put away between work sessions.

If a roller frame is to be used, center the fabric and carefully baste it to the webbing with heavy-duty thread. Adjust the rollers until the piece is taut. In some cases, it is also helpful to lace the side edges to the stretcher bars to insure a good taut fit. When working on this type of frame, loosen the tension on a roller slightly when the work is put away.

The artist's stretcher frame is very valuable for working pieces embellished with many long stitches or heavily textured stitches that should not have the hoop fastened on them. Purchase stretcher strips in the size of the finished piece. Center the fabric and pull the raw edges to the back of the frame, fastening them firmly with thumb tacks.

To work on a stretcher frame, prop it against a table edge or a chair arm so both hands are free to embroider. Usually it is best to begin working in the center of the design and work outward toward the edges.

Working on a hoop or frame insures even stitching, avoids puckering, and generally produces better embroidery. Working with one hand above and one below the hoop does take some small adjustment, but once the technique is mastered, the stitching becomes easier and progresses rapidly. Most people prefer to have the right hand under the hoop and the left on top to return the needle, but there is no reason this could not be reversed if it is more comfortable.

Some embroidery stitches can be worked neatly without a frame—indeed some teachers recommend that these stitches be worked without it—but others must have the firm taut background provided by the frame. For this reason, it is simplest to learn to work them all on the frame rather than to try to juggle the two methods.

Stitch charts traditionally show the needle inserted into the fabric as if the stitch were being worked without a frame. This is simply a pictorial step-saving device, and you will find it easy to follow the instructions with the fabric in the frame. If it is a stitch that is unfamiliar, follow the written directions step by step, bringing the needle to the surface where indicated, holding the yarn in position as shown, and proceeding as instructed. The photographs all show some completed stitches, as well as the one in the making. This should make it possible for even a beginner to learn the stitches from the book.

Read through the written working instructions for a project before beginning to work. Then follow the chart for stitch and color references and use the written hints for help with any areas that may be confusing. If a working order is included in the instructions, its use will usually speed the embroidery.

Length of Yarn

Work with short threads. Normally 12 inches to 15 inches is sufficient. Long strands wear thin and do not cover well.

If wool wears thin, even when a short length

is being used, check the needle. It may be a size too small, causing too much wear on the yarn as it is being pulled through the fabric. Some needles also have eyes shaped in such a way that they cut the yarn if too much pulling takes place. Keep an assortment of needles on hand and try several until you find the right one.

Working with the Twist of the Yarn

Each strand of wool yarn is made up of hundreds of short fibers spun into a continuous thread. If the strand is pulled through the thumb and forefinger, the grain or spinning direction can be felt. Pulled in one direction the thread is smooth, while the short fiber ends can be felt if the direction is reversed. The yarn should be threaded into the needle so the smooth side follows the needle into the fabric. This reduces abrasion and wear on the yarn and produces smoother embroidery.

Embroider Without Knots

Learn to embroider without knots. This is not the impossible task it may seem at first. Begin stitching on the right side with several small Running or Back Stitches in an area that will be covered with embroidery. Leave the end on the right side and cut it off when it is reached. Fas-

ten the end of a strand in the same manner. This method avoids knots, saves the time that would be spent turning the frame over to fasten ends, and eliminates loose ends hanging on the back. The ends can also be utilized as extra padding in Satin Stitch by holding them in place and working over them.

Covering Transfer Lines

Embroider slightly beyond the outlines of the design on the fabric to be certain the color from the transfer pencil is completely hidden. Work stitches slightly loose to allow the yarn to relax a little and to provide good coverage, especially in stitches worked solid to cover an area.

Embroidery Is Like Your Signature

Embroidery is very much like handwriting. Individual styles and variations are endless. You will develop your own as you learn and experiment. Practice and learn to work the stitches correctly, and then accept your own style just as you accept your signature,. Don't expect your work to look exactly like your neighbor's, friend's or teacher's. Do the best you can and then be proud to say it is your own, for it is exclusively yours.

STARTING CREWEL

In my beginning crewel class more than thirty years ago, I was given a piece of dull green denim and a few strands of black, dark green, and white yarn to work a stitch sampler. The teacher, a knowledgeable student of Americana and an unsurpassed instructor, nevertheless viewed learning the stitches as a lusterless ritual that had to be endured before one could begin to enjoy the embroidery process. She demonstrated each stitch both on the blackboard and on fabric and then painstakingly inspected each student's piece to make sure every detail was correct. This careful and personal attention took a great deal of time, and I remember being restless. I wanted to stitch and I wanted color—lots and lots of color and lots and lots of stitches—to bring to life the designs I had envisioned when I registered for the course.

But there was no hurrying our meticulous teacher, and we learned our stitches well—step by careful step; learned several methods of working each to achieve different effects; placed them neatly in little blocks on the green denim and lettered their names under them. When we had finally mastered about twenty-five stitches,

it was time to think about a project. The embroidery kit as we know it was not available in those days, so we were given a selection of tracings of historic pieces and were permitted to trace one. Next we transferred it to a fine creamy linen and chose yarns from a collection of lovely British crewels. Our vocabulary of twenty-five stitches was to be used as we thought best to complete the piece, and we were given permission to work a flower or two in the week's time before the next class. I was so excited I finished the whole piece that week!

My philosophy for working with beginners has come primarily from my experience in that class. Years of helping others get started with embroidery have enforced my belief that while there can be no substitute for good craftsmanship, the painstaking details necessary to learning can be combined with imagination to make the whole process exciting and fun. I know that we would have learned our stitches just as well on a piece of fine creamy linen and that the stitches themselves would have been much prettier and more inspiring in a few bright colors. Every beginner starts crewel embroidery because he has someway been touched by the gamut of color and texture that sets it apart from other embroideries, and he or she wants to begin to create it immediately.

There is no better way to master the stitches of crewel and to experience the feeling of making them with a wool thread than to make a simple stitch sampler. Most beginners want to create immediately but also want to make some type of practice piece that will bridge the gap between complete inexperience and confidence. Then, too, a sampler is an invaluable reference. My homely green one stayed in my workbasket for many years and was often used to get an idea of which stitch to use in my work or for a quick reminder of the texture a certain stitch would provide. It is still rolled in a drawer, a reminder of the beginning of my love affair with crewel.

The beginner who feels that the time spent on a sampler is wasted can learn on any number of small projects without sacrificing any basic skills because the sampler has been skipped. In this case, the choice of a first piece should be made carefully. It should be small enough to be completed in a relatively short time so the wonderful feeling of accomplishment can be experienced early. It should be attractive so there will be an incentive to finish. It must be of very good quality materials as these are the easiest to use. Instructions should be clear and very detailed.

For those who would like to begin with a stitch sampler, I have designed an informal piece that includes twenty-eight stitches including the ones designated as basic stitches (* after the name) in the Stitch Dictionary. It is an easy piece that can be framed as a picture, made up into a pillow, or simply kept in the workbasket as a reference. Complete instructions for making the sampler are included, but you may have your own ideas about layout, and you can certainly use them. For best results, choose a firmly woven linen or cotton fabric. Look for one with fairly even threads as the irregularities of a heavily textured fabric distort many stitches and make it difficult to see what is happening when a stitch is made. Cream color is best, but any light color will do. Choose a palette of pleasing and harmonious yarn colors, making sure you have four blending shades of one color to use for practice in shading. (Exact yarn colors are not listed to allow the use of odds and ends or to make a minimum purchase possible.)

A decorative and useful beginner project is the embroidered box on page 56. Not all of the basic stitch vocabulary has been used for the box cover, but the ones used have been arranged in an interesting style, and there are enough stitches for you to get a good feeling about embroidering with wool. The foundation box used is a small department store gift box. The linen is glued in place to make a neat little hideaway for trinkets. Again, you can follow instructions exactly or modify them to suit your needs.

The oval framed picture on page 60 was also designed as a beginner project. In the Colonial manner, it utilizes only seven stitches and is a practical and enjoyable way to get started. The design can be used for objects other than the picture, and the beginner may find it interesting to work the design several times using a selection of different stitches and colors to see the changes these alterations make.

Two pincushions on page 63 would also make good beginner pieces. They are small, use basic stitches, and are finished quickly.

Whichever avenue the beginner chooses, he will find that the instructions for the first projects are very detailed. Each project notes every step from the selection of fabric to the completion of the embroidery. Before starting, refer to the chapters dealing with materials and basic working instructions for help in these areas. The Stitch Dictionary deals with detailed instruction for the stitches, while other sections cover blocking, mounting, and other finishing details. If these are followed carefully, the new embroiderer will soon be producing beautiful crewel.

THE STITCHES

The study of embroidery stitches—the history and romance surrounding them, their geographic development and distribution, even their descriptive, sometimes colorful names—is a fascinating and absorbing hobby, for it has been estimated that there are more than three hundred stitches and variations of stitches. The list of stitches traditionally associated with crewel embroidery is considerably shorter but still extensive enough to lend almost infinite variety for creative expression. It is to these stitches that instructions are limited in this book, but keep in mind that while the stitches presented form an excellent working vocabulary and are sufficient for even ambitious projects, others may be added for variety or novelty. Many excellent stitch encyclopedias offer charts and working instructions for these additional stitches.

Instead of the familiar line drawings demonstrating stitch construction, the stitches are shown photographically as they are being worked. Each photograph shows a few completed stitches, the needle inserted as if to continue, with the thread always in proper position. The result is clear, almost graphic in detail. It is like having your teacher seated beside you demonstrating the stitch. Never again should you say, "I can't work from a book. I need someone to show me." That "someone" will always be as close as this book.

In the Stitch Dictionary, an asterisk (*) after the name of the stitch is a guide to the most useful and important stitches. These are not necessarily the easiest stitches but are the ones the beginner should learn first, as they are basic and are used most often in the projects in this book and in commercial embroidery kits. The three beginner projects (pages 52 to 62) make good use of most of these stitches, demonstrating their applicability, versatility, and textures.

To learn a new stitch, prepare the fabric in a frame or hoop, thread the needle, read the instructions for the stitch, and examine the photograph. Next, actually work the stitch, carefully following the written directions step by step. Check your work with the completed stitches shown on the photograph to make sure you have worked them correctly. The combination of written and pictorial instructions should make it possible for even the most inexperienced to learn new stitches easily.

The beginner often tends to work much too tightly, pulling the thread so the stitches do not cover the stamped lines and look thin and stretched. If this is your problem, try to relax. Don't rip out stitches already worked. Rather, continue to work. Usually tension slackens a little as you become more comfortable with the stitches, and the embroidery will visibly improve. Later, when the stitching has become more natural, it is possible to go back over the first stitches, working on top of them, using them as padding rather than cutting them out.

The most important objective when choosing stitches for a piece of embroidery is to use the stitches to best advantage, allowing them to enhance the design and to produce the overall effect the designer visualized. Sometimes an entire piece is worked most effectively in one stitch, other times two or three are sufficient, while still other pieces take advantage of dozens of different stitches. Choose carefully. The texture of the stitches, the size they are worked, and the way they are applied—heavy or light—can completely change the character and appearance of a piece of embroidery.

As you develop in skill, you will form a nucleus of favorite stitches and find that these are used as a basis for most of your projects. This becomes comfortable and results in a signature look in original designs. You may already have noticed it in your own work, and if you will read through the lists of stitches with the individual pieces in this book, you will quickly discover my staples.

This comfortable handling of stitches is found also in most historic pieces, the stitches having been determined both by the embroiderer's choice and the local custom. Eighteenth century English crewel was heavily worked, almost completely covering the background, and the list of stitches used is a long one. American crewel of the same period rarely contained more than four or five stitches, and these were usually used because they saved yarn. Outline, Roumanian Couching and Flat Stitches were favorites, but Chain, Buttonhole, French Knots, Seeding, Back Stitch and Surface Weaving were also often used. The charming blue and white Deerfield embroideries were worked in fifteen basic stitches and certainly did not suffer from lack of variety and interesting effects. In the historic pieces, as in today's, it is not the number of stitches used that determines the beauty of the embroidery, but the way in which the stitches are used.

Often the written stitch directions give hints about how the stitch can be used most effectively. It is helpful to know that a particular stitch is very good as an outline but can also be worked in close rows to fill a space entirely. Other little remarks found in the instructions are aimed at helping the reader to use the stitches in a variety of ways.

Large areas that need filling are a challenge, and there are many ways of handling them. Scattered stitches like Arrowhead, Seeding, Sheaf and Fly give a light open effect. Trellis Couching laid out in different patterns with the threads held in place by a variety of different stitches—Cross, Straight, Lazy Daisy—is an option that provides an interesting geometric pattern. Rows of Roumanian Couching, Chain, or Outline cover fabric completely with color and texture. French Knots can be scattered for an open look or worked close together to fill space completely. Ideas are unlimited and some of the options are shown on page 48. The single leaf worked eight ways on page 46 is another exercise in filling space that takes one shape and shows the changes that can be brought about by simply using different stitches.

Although the instructions for the projects in this book list exactly which stitches were used for the pictured model, feel free to experiment with others and thus personalize the designs. Buy a little extra yarn if you choose to try this as the substituted stitches may use more yarn, and you will undoubtedly do a little ripping out in the beginning. This experimentation is not possible with a kit because yarn is limited, but it is a feature of working from a book that should definitely be used to best advantage. Your finished pieces will not be exactly like the pictured models, but they will be partly your own creation, and for this reason, they will give you additional pleasure.

The Stitch Dictionary

ARROWHEAD STITCH

Can be used singly for scattered light filling, in rows as an outline, or in adjoining rows to make a geometric-patterned filling (See block 1 on Filling Ideas page).

To work: Bring the needle to the surface at *A* and pull the yarn through. Insert the needle at *B* bringing it out again at *C* (the three points form a triangle) and pull yarn through. Insert needle at *A* again and bring to surface at *D* pulling yarn through. Repeat, always inserting the needle in the hole formed by the adjacent stitch.

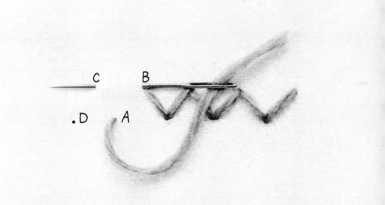

BACK STITCH*

An easy outline stitch, Back Stitch makes a neat line that bears a close resemblance to the top of a row of machine stitches. It may be used as a finishing edge or outline or can be worked in closely spaced rows to fill a large area. Worked very small, it is an ideal stitch for lettering and curved outlines. As a foundation outline under stitches like Satin and Fishbone, it adds padding and makes it easier to work the top stitch in a neat line.

To begin a row of stitches: Bring the needle to the surface at *A*, which is one stitch length from the beginning of the row, and pull the thread through. Go down at *B* and back to the surface at *C* keeping the distance from *A* to *B* and *A* to *C* equal. Pull the yarn through to form a stitch. Insert the needle again at *A* and continue stitching, keeping the stitches as uniform as possible.

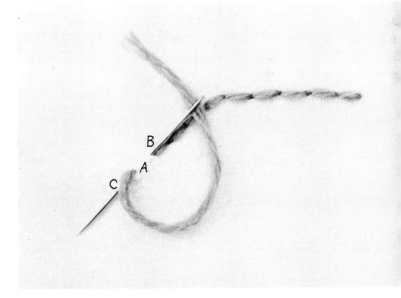

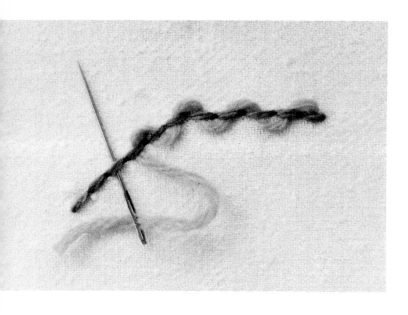

BACK STITCH, THREADED*

This is an easy way to make a two- or three-color line. The threading adds bulk to the fine line of the Back Stitch as well as color. The photograph shows only one thread being added to the row of Back Stitches, but a second can be added in the opposite direction to form picots in the alternate spaces.

Work a row of Back Stitch. Bring the needle to the surface near the center of the first stitch and pull yarn through. Without piercing the fabric, weave in and out under the stitches to form loops. Width of the line can be adjusted by the way loops are pulled up. Add a second row of loops if you like.

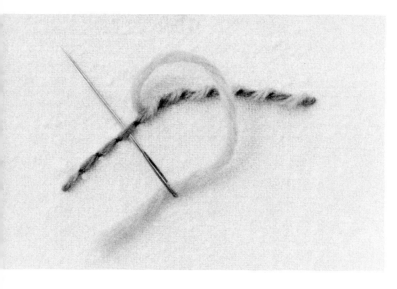

BACK STITCH, WHIPPED*

This embellishment of the Back Stitch adds another color without making the line much wider. It can be used in most situations where the plain Back Stitch would be appropriate.

Work a row of Back Stitch. Bring the needle to the surface near the center of the first stitch and pull the yarn through. Without piercing the fabric, whip along the row as shown.

BULLION KNOT*

Although it is a bit tricky at first, once mastered, the Bullion Knot is a much used stitch. It can be made to lie flat along a line, or to curve, or to form a rosebudlike cluster. Its coiled length makes an interesting raised flower center, or it can be used as a detail in many different situations.

To begin: Bring the needle up at A and pull the yarn through. Go down at B and come up again at A but do not pull the thread through. Wrap the yarn around the needle until the length of the coil is roughly the distance from A to B.

Hold the wrap firmly and pull the needle through the coil of yarn. Hold the wrap and pull the yarn all the way through so the stitch lies flat on the fabric. Take the needle to the wrong side at B.

If the yarn is wrapped around the needle so the coil is the same length as the distance from A to B, the stitch will lie flat on the fabric. To make a curved stitch, wrap the yarn around the needle a few more times and proceed in the same manner.

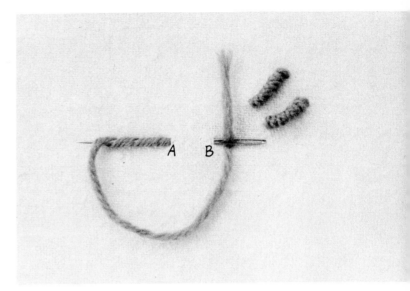

BUTTONHOLE STITCH, OPEN*

Sometimes called the Blanket Stitch, Buttonhole can be worked with the loops widely and evenly spaced, as shown in the photograph, or in many variations that group the stitches in decorative patterns. When the stitches are placed close together, they become an effective filling with a slightly raised edge.

To work: Bring the needle up at A and pull the yarn through. Holding the yarn above the needle to form a loop, insert the needle into the fabric at B and bring it back to the surface at C. Pull the needle through, adjusting the tension of the loop to allow the stitch to lie flat. Continue in this manner.

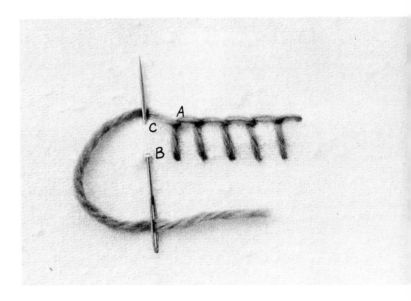

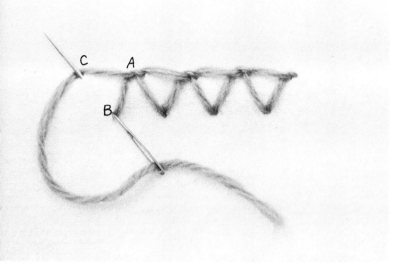

BUTTONHOLE, CLOSED

This variation of the Buttonhole makes a pretty edge. Work as for Open Buttonhole, but slant the stitches to *B* so they form the triangular shape. Always use the same hole at *B* to make a neat row.

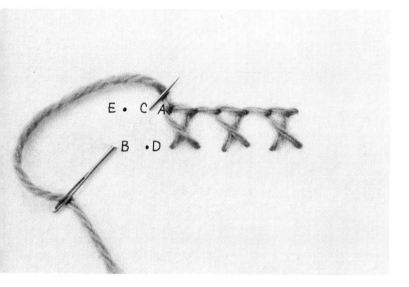

BUTTONHOLE, CROSSED

The long arms of this Buttonhole edge are crossed to make an interesting pattern. Work like Open Buttonhole, but make the length from *A* to *B* longer so the stitch will slant. Bring the needle to the surface at *C* and pull the yarn through. Insert the needle at *D* and bring it to the surface at *E* to form the Cross Stitch.

CHAIN STITCH*

A single row of Chain Stitch forms a broad outline, while closely spaced rows following the form of a motif make an effective filling stitch.

To start: Bring the needle up at *A* pulling the yarn through. Holding the thread below the needle to form a loop, insert the needle again at *A* and bring the needle up at *B*. Pull yarn through and adjust the loop.

When working rows as a filling, begin by outlining the outside edge of the motif, and then work concentric rows toward the center, maintaining the same direction for all rows and allowing the rows to flow in the same lines as the shape being filled. In the center, fill any small section that will not accommodate full rows with the portions of rows that fit.

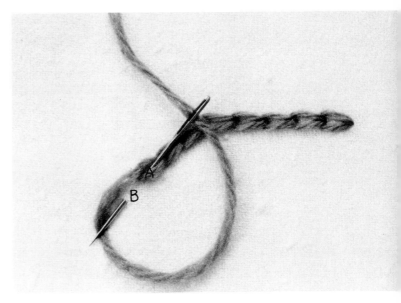

CHAIN STITCH, INTERLACED

There are many variations of the Chain Stitch. This one adds a second color by interlacing a thread under the foundation chain.

To work: First make a row of Chain Stitch. With a matching or contrasting color in the needle, come to the surface at the middle and slightly under the first chain. Then, without piercing the fabric, weave back and forth under the stitches, leaving the loops of color an even length. If you like, you may add another course of weaving in the opposite direction.

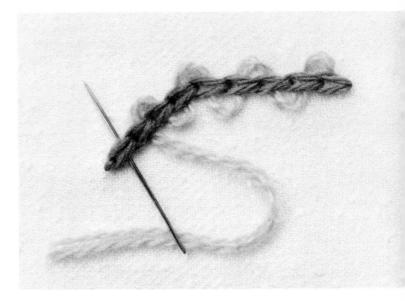

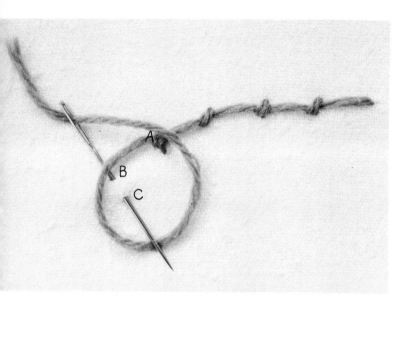

CORAL STITCH*

Coral Stitch was a favorite among Early American embroiderers; several beautiful pieces worked almost completely in its pretty knotted outlines have been found. The knots can be spaced differently as needed. The stitch can be worked as a filling by working closely spaced rows in which the knots are alternated so that one falls in the space between the knots of the adjoining row.

To begin: Bring the yarn up at A and pull through. Lay the yarn along the stitching line to the left and make a loop as shown. Hold in place with the thumb. Insert the needle at B and bring to surface at C, making a small slanting stitch. With lower part of loop under needle, pull yarn through to form a knot. Continue from beginning.

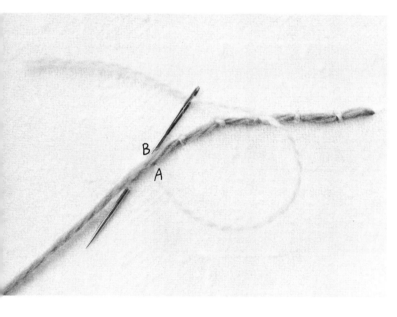

COUCHING*

Couching, actually a method of fastening down long threads on the surface of the embroidery, appears in many variations and fills many needs. It can make a delicate outline or any one of a dozen decorative fillings.

To work: Hold the thread to be fastened—the laid thread, shown as the darker thread on the photograph—in position along the line to be worked. Bring the needle, threaded with another strand (either the same color or a contrasting one), to the surface at A and insert it again at B on the other side of the laid thread. Pull through, forming the small stitch that fastens the thread in place. These little Couching Stitches may be upright or slightly slanted as desired.

Rows of this form of Couching can also be used as a solid filling. When this is done, place the small stitches carefully as they form a secondary pattern that can add greatly to the appearance of the embroidery.

CROSS STITCH*

Equally at home on canvas or fabric, the Cross Stitch is very easy but nonetheless beautiful and effective. The secret of perfect Cross Stitch is always to have the base stitches slanting in one direction throughout the work. When making multiple stitches in one color, it is best to work across making the base stitches (shown by the slanted stitch A to B in the photograph) and then return, placing the second stitches on top as shown. Single stitches can be completed individually.

To work a row of stitches: Bring the needle to the surface at A and pull yarn through. Insert needle at B and bring it up again at C which is directly below B and to the right on the same line as A. Pull yarn through to form the slanted stitch. Continue to the end of the row. Return by working as shown by the needle inserting it and bringing it to the surface in the same holes made by the previous stitches.

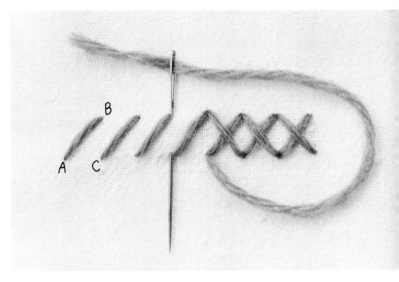

ERMINE STITCH

This nice textured stitch for filling or borders consists of a long Straight Stitch with an elongated Cross Stitch on top.

To work: Bring the needle up at A and pull yarn through. Insert the needle at B and come up again at C pulling the yarn through. Insert the needle at D above and to the right of the base of the long stitch. Bring it up at E in corresponding position on the left of the long stitch. Pull yarn through. Take the needle to the back at F to complete the stitch. Note that the base of the cross is narrower than the top.

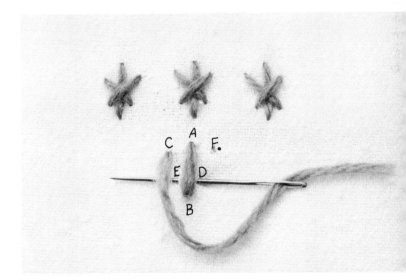

27

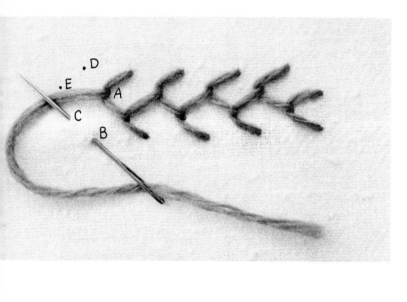

FEATHER STITCH

Feather Stitch is lovely for lines, outlines, fernlike leaves, even fillings. Work from right to left or top to bottom.

To begin: Bring the needle to the surface at *A* and pull yarn through. Lay yarn flat and hold in place with thumb. Insert needle at *B* and bring it up at *C* with the loop of yarn in the position shown on the photograph. Pull the yarn through. Holding the yarn flat again and making the loop in the opposite direction, insert the needle on the opposite side at *D* and bring it out again at *E* and pull through to form a loop. Repeat to desired length.

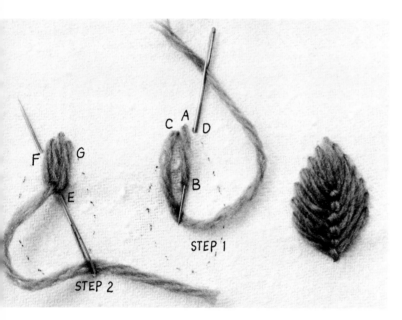

FISHBONE STITCH*

The Fishbone Stitch is ideal filling for many floral forms and is thus a very much used crewel stitch. It can be worked solid (as in the photograph) or with the stitches widely spaced for an open look. The first stitch should be fairly long to insure that the side stitches lie on a good slant.

To begin: Bring the needle up at *A*, pull the yarn through and go down at *B* which is about ¼ inch down the center line from *A*. Come up at *C* which is to the left and very slightly below *A* on the outline. Holding the thread below the needle to form a loop go down at *D*, which corresponds to *C* but is to the right of *A*. Bring the needle to the surface again at *B* and pull the yarn through, adjusting the loop so the stitch lies flat (end of step 1 in photograph).

Make a small stitch across the loop by inserting the needle at *E* as shown in step 2. Come up at *F* on the left side and repeat the loop-forming and tie-down stitch until the area is covered.

28

FLAT STITCH

As a solid filling stitch, Flat can often be substituted for Satin and Roumanian Couching. It is a good stitch that provides texture and fills large areas quickly. The stitches in the photograph are spaced far apart to show stitch construction. Flat may also be worked close together to cover fabric.

To begin: Bring the needle up at A and pull the yarn through. Go down at B and up again at C pulling the yarn through again. With yarn above the needle, go in at D and out again at E, noting the horizontal position of the needle. Pull the yarn through. Throw yarn to left and above the needle again, and insert the needle at F as shown in step 2. Bring needle out at G, noting the needle position again. Throw yarn to right above the needle and repeat step 1 as shown in the photograph, omitting the long stitch from A to B. Repeat the two steps until the area is filled.

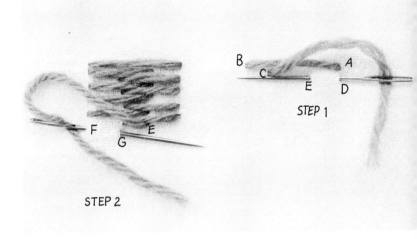

FLY STITCH

Fly Stitch is usually used as a light filling, but can be worked in rows as a border or in adjoining rows to make a geometric-patterned filling. The tie-down stitch can be made any length as needed.

To begin: Bring the needle up at A pulling the thread through. With the yarn in the position shown, go down at B and up at C. Pull the yarn through and adjust the loop so it lies flat but is not stretched. Make a small tie-down stitch over the loop.

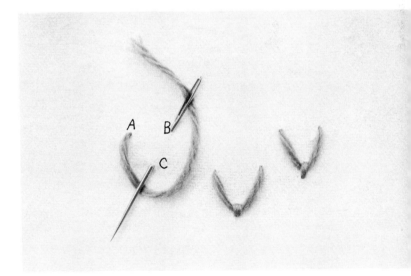

29

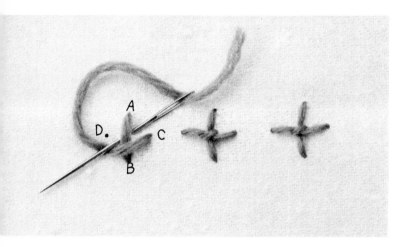

FOUR-LEGGED KNOT

This is an interesting knotted stitch usually used as a scattered filling. Keep the knot fairly loose for best results.

To make a knot: Bring the needle to the surface at *A* and pull the yarn through. Go down at *B* and come back up at *C* pulling thread through. With yarn in position shown and without piercing the fabric, slide the needle under the vertical stitch. Pull yarn through to make a knot. Take needle to back of work at *D*.

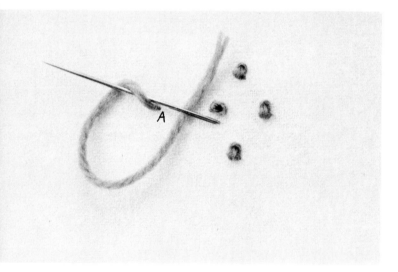

FRENCH KNOT*

This interesting little knot serves many purposes; indeed, it would be hard to imagine embroidery without the charm of French Knots. They can be used singly as seeding, packed together to form solid textured areas, worked in rows of shaded colors, or grouped to make interesting flower centers and other floral details.

To make the knot: Bring the needle to the surface at *A* and pull the yarn through. Wrap the yarn around the needle once; then insert the tip of the needle into the fabric close to *A* but with at least one thread intervening. Pull the yarn to tighten the loop snugly around the needle. Pull the needle through to the back of the work.

FRENCH KNOT ON A LONG STEM

This is a useful little detail stitch that can be worked to form flower centers, miniature trees, leaves, and can be a tacking stitch for Trellis Couching.

To begin: Bring the needle to the surface at *A* and pull the yarn through. Wrap the yarn around the needle once. Insert the tip of the needle into the fabric at *B* and pull the yarn to tighten the wrap around the needle. Pull needle to the back of the work.

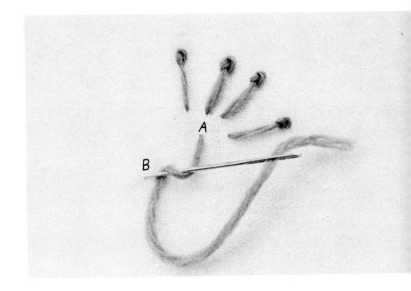

HERRINGBONE STITCH

Herringbone is good for wide lines, borders, and as a filling stitch. Work from left to right. Try some of the variations: Double is one, or try adding a Back Stitch in contrasting color at the intersection of the crosses on legs, or try interlacing or whipping with another color.

Begin at left by bringing the yarn to the surface at *A* and pulling through. With the yarn in the position shown, insert the needle at *B* and bring it out at *C*. Pull through. Throw yarn to top, insert the needle at *D*, and bring it to the surface at *E*. Repeat to complete row.

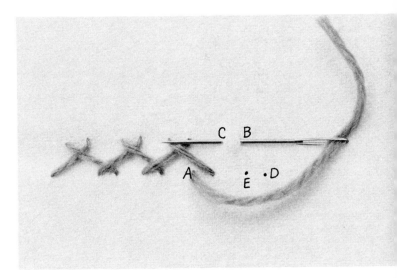

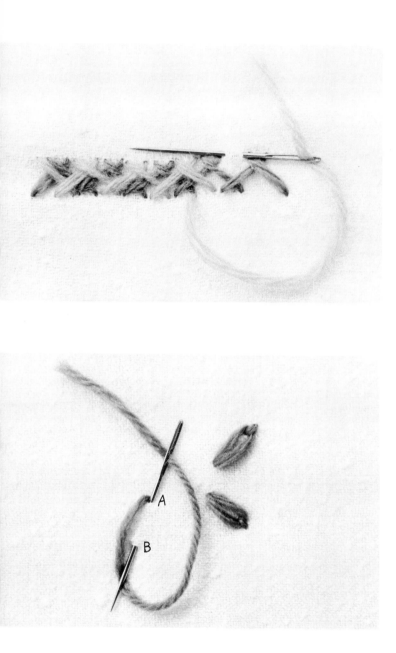

HERRINGBONE, DOUBLE

Work a row of single Herringbone, following the directions. With another color work a second row, placing the short stitches between the ones of the first row.

LAZY DAISY STITCH*

The Lazy Daisy is often called the Detached Chain, which is a very accurate description of it. This is an easy stitch that can be used for many small details, makes lovely little flowers and leaves, can fasten Trellis Couching threads, or add variety to other Couching patterns that need filling stitches.

To work: Bring the needle up at A and pull the yarn through. Holding the yarn below the needle to form a loop, go down again at A and bring the needle to the surface at B. Pull the yarn through and adjust the loop. Make a small stitch across the loop at B to fasten.

LONG AND SHORT STITCH*

Any list of basic crewel stitches would certainly have Long and Short on it, for this stitch produces shading and detail unequaled by any other. It may be worked in even rows or in an irregular pattern that causes a painted effect. The basic stitching foundation is the same for the two methods.

Only the first or outside row has both Long and Short Stitches, a quirk that is often confusing to the beginner. To practice the stitch, use a heavy yarn and work the rows in shades of one color, beginning with the darkest at the outside and working through the tones to the lightest.

Begin with a straight edge and make the long stitches ½ inch and the short ones ¼ inch. Work a short row, placing the stitches close together as shown in the photograph. Change to the next lighter tone, and work a row of long stitches in the slotted spaces by bringing the needle to the surface through the yarn at the base of each short stitch. Change to a lighter color and work the row of long stitches in the spaces produced by the last row. The delicate shading pattern will emerge by this time, but you can continue shading further if you wish.

To work a curved line: Begin the outside row at the middle of the curve and work the Long and Short Stitches to one side, then go back to the center and work to the other side. Stitches should overlap slightly and change direction to fit an irregular shape.

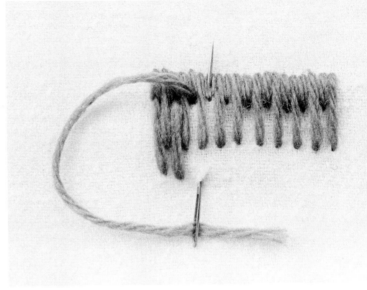

An outline of Split Stitch around a motif to be worked in Long and Short will impart a raised appearance and a very smooth edge.

When Long and Short is used in this book, all the colors in the shaded area are listed in the order to be worked in the motif on the chart. Thus, a flower petal marked to be in Long and Short in colors 855, 860, and 865 would be worked, shading the colors from light to dark, using the three shades of color noted. Use the color photographs as a guide to shading and handle the colors much as paint to achieve a delicate transition from one value to the next.

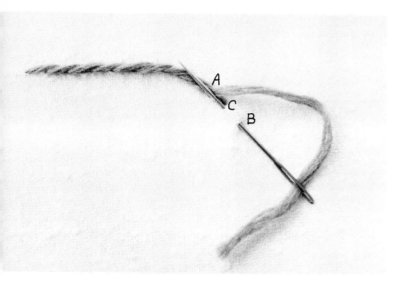

OUTLINE STITCH*

Worked as shown in the photograph, with the yarn always above the needle, the Outline Stitch creates a fine line of very close stitches. When the yarn is thrown below the needle, the line is perceptibly broader, and the stitches are slightly separated. Some embroiderers call the fine line the Stem Stitch and the broad one the Crewel Stitch, but in fact, they are both the Outline.

To begin a line of stitching: Bring the needle to the surface at *A* and pull the yarn through. With the yarn above the needle, go down at *B* and come up at *C* exactly halfway between *A* and *B*. Pull the yarn through and continue stitching.

OUTLINE STITCH, INTERLACED

Outline Stitch can be widened, and one or two colors can be added by interlacing another strand (or strands) in and out under the completed stitches.

To begin: Bring the yarn to the surface at the center and slightly under the first stitch. Without piercing the fabric, weave the yarn in and out to form picots as shown in the photograph. If you want a second color, bring the yarn up again under the first stitch and weave in the opposite direction.

OUTLINE STITCH, WHIPPED

To add a second color and still maintain a fine line of Outline Stitch: Whip a completed row of Outline with another strand of yarn. Bring the needle up at the end of the row, and with the yarn in position shown, slide the needle under the stitches without piercing the fabric.

PEKINGESE STITCH

Pekingese is actually an embellishment of the Back Stitch and because of the loops is best used as a single line. It is a very decorative stitch which looks much like an ornamental braid.

First work a row of Back Stitch, keeping it even and fairly small. Use matching or contrasting color for the loops, which have been exaggerated in the photograph to show construction.

To begin looping: Bring the needle up just below the first Back Stitch. Without piercing the fabric, slide the needle up under the second Back Stitch, pulling the yarn through and leaving a small loop. Then slide the needle downward under the first Back Stitch. Bring the needle out under the loop made by the first stitch. Leave a small loop at the top of the row of Back Stitching. Next slide the needle upward under the third Back Stitch and downward under the second Back Stitch, leaving a loop each time. Repeat this rhythm to end of row.

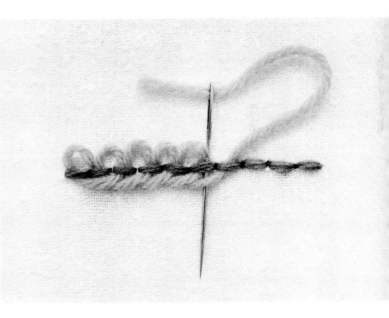

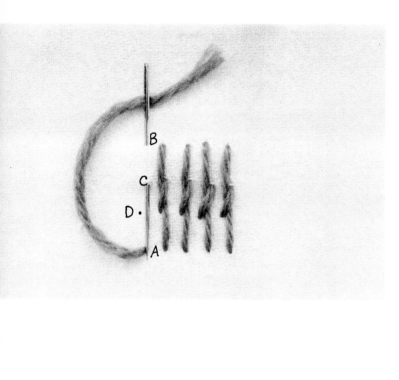

ROUMANIAN COUCHING*

Roumanian Couching was a great favorite among Colonial embroiderers for it fills an area with solid color much as Satin but requires much less yarn. It is found row upon row on petticoat borders, chair seats, and bed hangings, testimony to its enduring beauty.

Use Roumanian Couching anywhere a solid filling is needed. Work in rows, overlapping them just slightly so no fabric shows between the bands. Shading can be accomplished by working successive rows in graduated shades of one color.

The stitches shown in the photograph are widely spaced to show construction better. They should be worked close together to form a solid filling. Keep the slant of the small tie-down stitch as shown so the long stitches will lie close together.

To begin: Bring the needle to the surface at *A* and pull yarn through. Holding yarn as shown, go down at *B* and up at *C*; pull yarn through to form a long flat stitch. Make a slanting tie-down stitch by going down at *D* on the other side of the long stitch, and bring the needle up again next to *A* to begin next stitch.

RUNNING STITCH*

Running Stitch is a basic sewing stitch, good also for embroidery when a fine light line is needed. Can also be worked back and forth in rows to make a light filling.

Work as shown in the photograph, keeping the length of the stitches on top of the fabric longer than those on the back. Try to maintain an even stitch length.

RUNNING STITCH, INTERLACED

Interlacing gives a chained look to Running Stitch and perceptibly widens it. One or two colors may be added as the interlacing threads. It may also be worked with only one row of interlacing as shown on the left side of the photograph.

To begin: Bring the needle up just under and at the center of the first Running Stitch. Without piercing the fabric, slide the needle downward under the second Running Stitch. Change directions and slide the needle upward under the next stitch and adjust loop. Continue across the row, always alternating the direction of the needle.

To add a second color, bring the needle up just under and at the center of the first Running Stitch and work across the row, filling in the alternate spaces left by the first row.

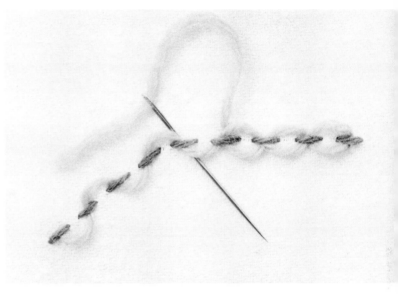

RUNNING STITCH, WHIPPED*

This is a very quick decorative two-color line stitch. First work a row of Running Stitch. With another color yarn, bring the needle up just under the center of the first Running Stitch. With yarn in position and without piercing the fabric, slide the needle upward under the second Running Stitch. Continue along the row, always inserting the needle upward with the yarn in the position shown.

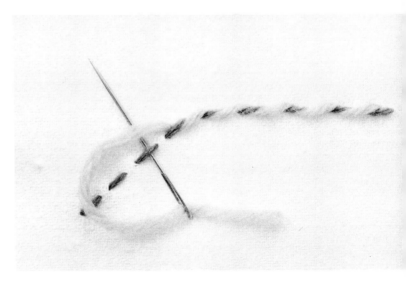

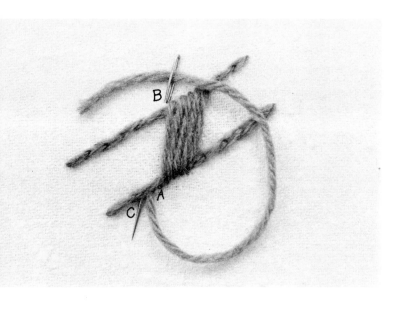

SATIN STITCH*

One of the loveliest of embroidery stitches, Satin is aptly named, for when properly worked it has a smooth, lustrous look. A Split Stitch outline underneath adds depth and eases the task of making an even outside edge. Extra padding in the form of long stitches can be added. Most of the Satin Stitch in the projects in this book has been worked over the foundation padding of Split Stitch as shown in the photograph.

To work as photographed: Outline the area with small Split Stitch in the same color that will be used for the Satin Stitch. Begin the Satin Stitch by bringing the needle to the surface at A and pulling the yarn through. Make a slanting stitch by taking the needle down at B and bringing it up again at C which is close to A. Pull yarn through and continue stitching until area is covered.

On the charts for the projects, you will find small arrows that indicate the slant of Satin Stitches. These are to be used as a guide in placing the stitches.

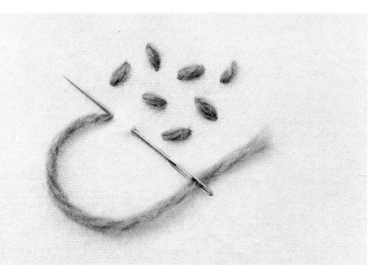

SEEDING*

Seeding is ideal as a light filling for flowers, leaves, even backgrounds where just a light texture and a little color is needed.

To work: Make tiny straight stitches and place them at random. The ones shown in the photograph are made double—two stitches in each space. This makes them nice and plump and a little raised. Single stitches can also be used when a lighter texture is needed.

SHEAF STITCH

Sheaf—sometimes called Bundle—is generally used as a filling stitch. It adds a definite pattern and so should be placed in areas that can stand the addition.

Construction of the stitch is easy. Begin by making three long flat parallel stitches. Bring the needle up beneath the center stitch. Slide the needle under the left stitch and with yarn in the position shown, take the needle under the stitch on the right and to the back of the work under the center stitch. Pull the gathering stitch tight enough to bind the stitches into the sheaf.

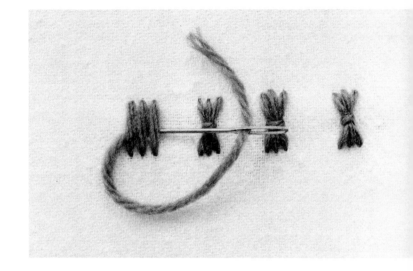

SPIDER WEB, WHIPPED*

Spider Web is usually worked within a circular area. It is a fascinating stitch—fun to work and fun to use imaginatively. It is a raised stitch so it adds a great deal of texture and makes perfect flower centers and other circular details. It can be worked with the spokes completely covered or partially exposed. More than one color can be used, so it is possible to shade or contrast within one stitch.

To begin: Place the spokes of the wheel following the letters in step 1. Next bring the needle to the surface as close as possible to the center of the spokes in the space between E and D. Without piercing the fabric, slide the needle under two spokes (D and H), as shown in the photograph, and pull the yarn through. Now slide the needle under spokes H and A and pull yarn through. Yarn has wrapped around spoke H. Repeat, sliding under A and F. Continue around the wheel, always going under one new spoke and the one immediately preceding it. See step 2. Continue until stitch is desired fullness. The more trips around the wheel, the higher the stitch will be.

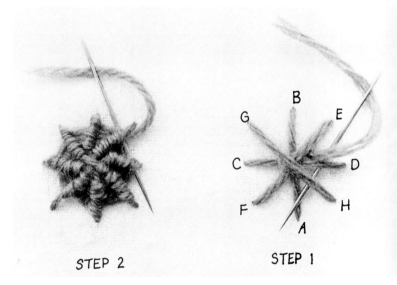

STEP 2   STEP 1

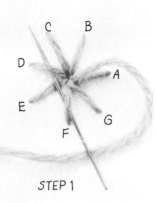

STEP 2

STEP 1

SPIDER WEB, WOVEN

The Woven Spider Web is not quite as raised as the Whipped but has a distinctive appearance and can be used in much the same way.

Because it is woven and must be worked on an uneven number of spokes, the foundation is laid out as shown in step 1 with seven spokes that all end in a center hole. Place them as shown in the photograph, spacing them evenly. Next, bring the needle to the surface, as close as possible to the center of the stitch, in the space between spokes A and G. Pull yarn through. Now without piercing the fabric, simply weave round and round the wheel—over one, under one, etc.—until stitch is the fullness desired. As with the Whipped version, the spokes may be left partially exposed or may be completely covered.

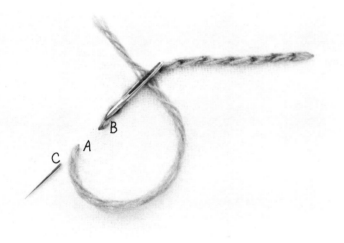

SPLIT STITCH *

Hardworking little Split Stitch, which looks like a scaled-down version of Chain Stitch, does many embroidery jobs. It is a lovely fine outlining stitch, is often used as a padding under other stitches, and can be worked in closely spaced rows as a solid filling.

To start: Bring the needle up at A and pull the yarn through. Go down at B and up at C, keeping the space between A and C equal to that between A and B. Pull thread through, forming a small flat stitch between A and B. Insert the needle down into the center of this stitch, splitting it as shown in the photograph. Continue across the row.

STAR STITCH*

Star is an individual motif stitch that is good for light filling and circular details. Based on a circle, the foundation is three long stitches that cross in the center. Place them as shown in the photograph, following the letters as a guide to sequence. Next, bring the needle to the surface at *G,* which is as close as possible to the center, and in the space between spokes *A* and *C.* Pull yarn through and take the needle to the back of the work at *H* to form the tie-down.

STRAIGHT STITCH*

The Straight Stitch is an uncomplicated flat stitch often used as an accent or scattered as seeding to add texture to a large, otherwise plain area. The slant and size of the stitches can vary to suit the need.

To work: Simply place the stitches at the desired angle, following the stitching order from *A* to *B* to *C.*

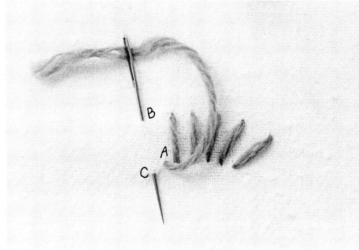

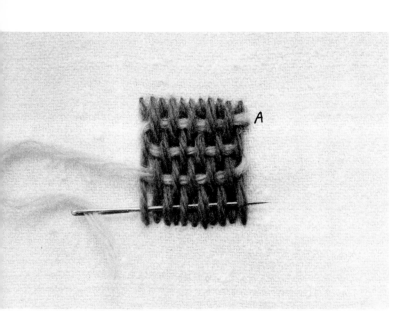

SURFACE DARNING (WEAVING) *

This stitch has been aptly named for it is exactly the stitch we once used for darning socks, but in embroidery there is no hole underneath! The woven effect is lovely filling for many motifs, and the pattern of the weaving can be altered by changing the number of threads crossed over and under.

To work: Lay a foundation of an uneven number of long vertical stitches to fill the area or motif. Using contrasting or matching yarn, bring the needle to the surface at *A* and pull yarn through. Weave the needle over one foundation thread, under the next, over the next, etc., to end of row. Pull yarn through. Work the return row, weaving under the threads that were crossed over, over the threads that were under in the previous row. Continue until area is woven.

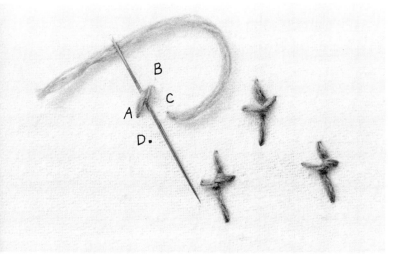

SWORD STITCH

Usually used as an isolated individual stitch for scattered filling, Sword can also be lined up with the horizontal bars touching to form a border. The slightly raised detail is a good addition to the embroiderer's repertoire of stitches.

To begin: Bring the needle to the surface at *A* and pull the thread through. Insert the needle at *B* and come up at *C* and pull through loosely. Without piercing the background fabric, slide the needle under the loose stitch between *A* and *B*, holding the yarn and needle as in the photograph. Pull through to form the knotted horizontal bar. Finish by taking the needle to the back at *D* and adjusting the horizontal stitch. For best results, leave the stitch from *A* to *B* slack enough to be pulled down to the center by the knot.

TÊTE DE BOEUF

Translated, Tête de Boeuf means Head of the Bull, certainly an accurate name for this unusual stitch. The size of the loop "ears" can be changed to make interesting variations. Use as a scattered filling or in rows as a border.

Step 1 makes the open loop for the ears. Begin by bringing the needle to the surface at *A* and pulling the yarn through. With the yarn in position under the needle as shown in the photograph, go down at *B* and up at *C*. Pull through to form loop but do not draw tight. Insert the needle again at *C* and bring it out again at *D* as in step 2. Arrange the yarn under the needle to form a loop as shown and pull through. Adjust the loop and make a small tacking stitch over the loop at *D* but on the other side of the loop to hold it in place.

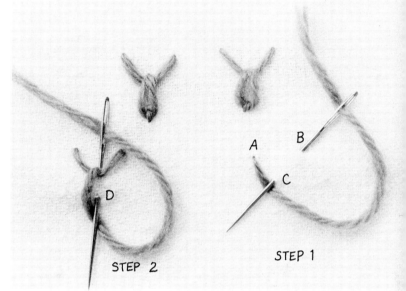

STEP 2   STEP 1

TRELLIS COUCHING*

Trellis Couching quickly covers a large area with interesting pattern. The laid and couching threads can be of matching color or of contrasting color. The latter may take the simple upright form shown in the photograph, or may be Cross Stitch, Lazy Daisy, or any one of a number of small stitches that would hold the threads in place. The diamond-shaped openings can be left plain as shown, or may be decorated with a small detached stitch.

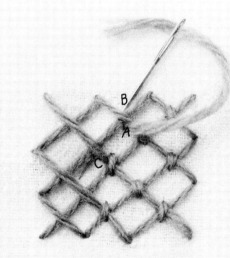

To begin: Lay the long Straight Stitches in diagonal parallel lines, filling the shape of the motif. Bring the needle threaded with the couching yarn to the surface at *A* and pull the yarn through. Make the tie-down stitch by inserting the needle at *B* and bringing it up again at *C* in position for the beginning of the next stitch. Tie each intersection of the laid threads.

When Trellis Couching is used in the projects in this book, dual numbers separated by a slash (/) on the chart indicate that the thread to be laid is of the first color while the tie-down stitches are of the second color. See page 48 for Couching Stitch ideas.

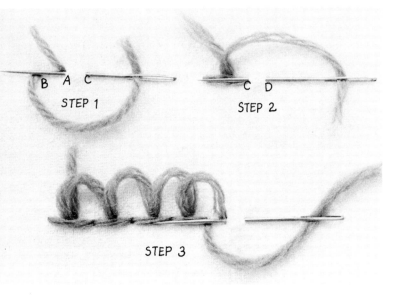

STEP 1

STEP 2

STEP 3

TURKEY WORK

Turkey Work makes fuzzy little animals, plump cattails, loop flowers, and many other sculptured forms with velvety texture. Loops can be cut, then brushed to look like thick velvet or can be left uncut. Always work in horizontal rows and make the loops the best length for the shape being filled.

To begin as in step 1: Insert the needle from the right side at *A* and pull yarn through to the back, leaving a short tail of yarn on the top. Bring the needle to the surface at *B* and pull through. With yarn under the needle as shown, insert the needle at *C* and bring it up at *A*. Pull yarn through to form a stitch. With the yarn above the needle as in step 2, insert the needle at *D* and bring it up at *C*. Pull yarn through, leaving a loop of the desired length. Repeat step 1 with yarn below the needle to form the flat stitch (which knots the loop in place). Repeat step 2 with yarn above the needle to form a loop. Alternate these two steps across the row as shown in step 3.

WHEAT EAR

Good for borders, stems, and isolated filling, Wheat Ear is a composite of two Straight Stitches and a detached Chain Stitch.

To begin step 1: Bring the needle to the surface at *A* and pull the yarn through. Insert the needle at *B* and come up again at *A*; pull yarn through. Insert the needle at *C*, come up again at *A* and pull through. Insert the needle at *A* as shown in step 2 and come up at *D*, making a loop around the needle to the right as shown. Pull yarn through and adjust the loop. Make a short tacking stitch by taking the needle to the back of the work on the other side of the loop at *D*.

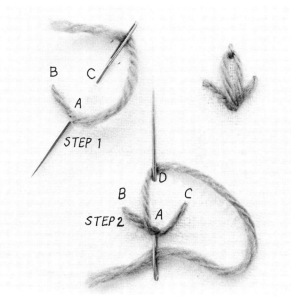

STEP 1

STEP 2

One Leaf—Eight Effects with Stitches

Although the finished projects in the Portfolio of Designs are complete with material lists and instructions for duplicating them exactly, you may feel you want to experiment with stitches of your own choice. This allows for a great deal of creativity and is one of the biggest advantages of working from a book.

To illustrate the variety of effects possible, the adjoining page shows one leaf worked eight different ways. A palette of five shades of green was handled differently for each leaf—some are fanciful, others more realistic; some are worked in all five of the greens while others contain only one or two; shading and filling methods vary and the stitches employed emphasize different parts of the leaf. Although eight are shown, there are many more possibilities. If you have worked a stitch sampler and have thus developed a feeling for the way stitches "work up," you already have many ideas on ways to develop this process further.

Leaf 1. The "painted" shading of this leaf is achieved with the Long and Short Stitch and all five shades of green, beginning with the palest at the tip and working up to the darkest at the top. The stems of all leaves are worked in Satin Stitch.

Leaf 2. Hundreds of tiny French Knots and all five shades of green give this leaf interesting texture. When using French Knots as a filling, as shown here, work them very close together so none of the background fabric shows through.

Leaf 3. A leaf Mother Nature would never recognize is sprinkled with Satin Stitch dots and edged with a single row of Outline Stitch in the same shade of green as was used for the dots.

Leaf 4. This pale leaf is worked in four of the greens, using a greater portion of the lightest shade and a very small amount of the darkest tone. The Roumanian Couching Stitch is good for this effect, adding texture as well as graduated shading.

Leaf 5. Padded Satin Stitch in two shades of green with an Outline Stitch vein makes a realistic leaf. Note the way the slanted Satin Stitches meet at the vein.

Leaf 6. Trellis Couching and Outline Stitch make an elegant Jacobean leaf. The outside edge is bounded by two rows of Outline in the two darkest greens while medium green laid threads of the Couching are held in place with tiny stitches of the palest tone. A small Seed Stitch of the medium green fills the center of each diamond-shaped opening.

Leaf 7. Another Jacobean-style leaf is worked with scattered French Knots, Outline and Buttonhole Stitches all in one shade of green.

Leaf 8. Rows of closely spaced Chain Stitch using all five shades of green make a pretty leaf. The rows of stitching following the shape emphasize the flowing lines of the motif and quickly fill the space with simple shading.

ONE LEAF—EIGHT EFFECTS WITH STITCHES

Space to Fill—Eleven Ideas

Block 1. Arrowhead Stitch—eight rows of it worked so all stitches join—makes a diamond grid that quickly fills the space with pattern. French Knots in contrasting color add interest.

Block 2. Randomly scattered French Knots fill a space with texture and color.

Block 3. Trellis Couching is always a good choice for filling large areas. It is quick, pretty, and easily varied. Here it is tied down with upright Cross Stitches in contrasting color.

Block 4. Trellis Couching laid out in a pattern of squares has Sword Stitch in the center of each square and a small diagonal tie-down stitch.

Block 5. A large area is laid out in square Trellis Couching. Four Lazy Daisy Stitches in the alternate squares are the tie-down stitches but are also a major part of the pattern. Contrasting color French Knots center each flower and also the alternate squares.

Block 6. Again the square-patterned Trellis Couching, this time with Cross Stitch tie-down threads and a Lazy Daisy flower in the center of alternate blocks.

Block 7. Fly Stitch, French Knots and Straight Stitches fill a square with quick, easy pattern.

Block 8. Trellis Couching laid out in squares has a Sheaf Stitch in each square and a contrasting color Cross Stitch for tie-downs.

Block 9. Fairly close threads of Trellis Couching laid out in squares is ornamented simply with contrasting color and diagonal tie-down threads.

Block 10. Seeding, all one color and scattered at random, is an easy way to add texture and just a little color to an area.

Block 11. Trellis Couching laid out in small diamonds is a pretty filling. This is tied with small upright stitches in a contrasting color.

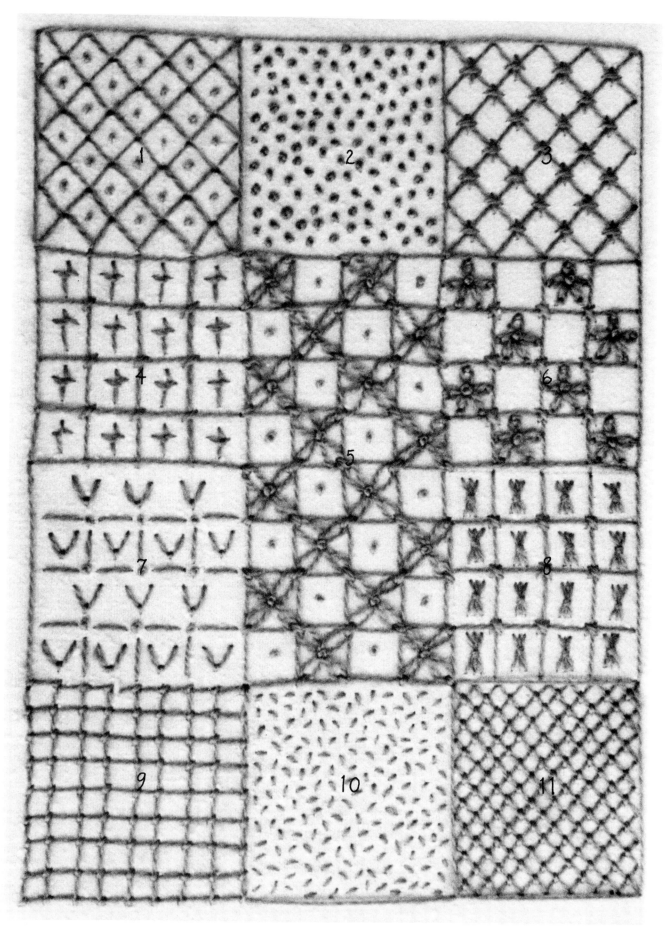

SPACE TO FILL—ELEVEN IDEAS

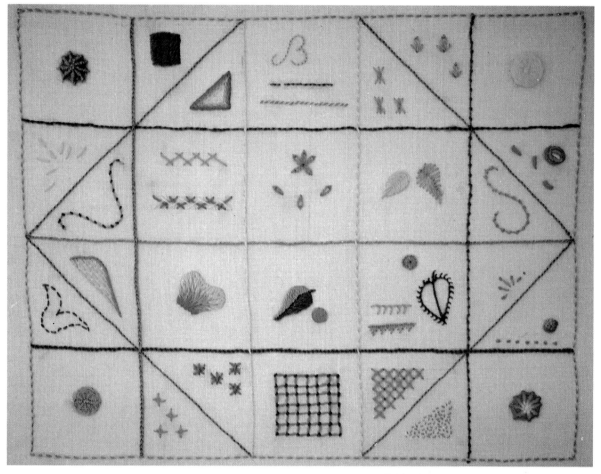

BEGINNER STITCH SAMPLER, page 52

EMBROIDERED BOX, page 56

OVAL PICTURE, page 61

LACE-EDGED ROUND PINCUSHION,
page 67

DAISY PILLOW, page 69

LACE-EDGED SQUARE PINCUSHION,
page 65

BRIDAL PILLOW, page 71

JUSTIN, page 72

KIRSTEN, page 72

JUSTIN (Detail), page 76

KIRSTEN (Detail), page 74

BELL PULL, page 88

FOUR FLOWERS PILLOW, page 94

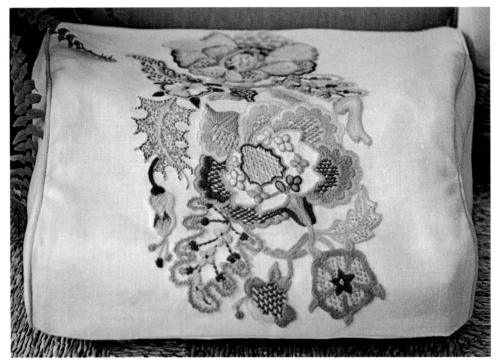

TYPEWRITER COVER, page 103

MINI-PANEL, page 84

JAPANESE LADIES, page 115

MODERN JACOBEAN PILLOW, page 79

PEACOCK PICTURE, page 131

PICTURE FRAME, page 113

TULIP EYEGLASS CASE, page 101

TOOTH FAIRY PILLOW, page 122

ABC PILLOW, page 134

DRAWSTRING POUCH, page 109

WHITE WOOL AFGHAN, page 125

WHITE WOOL AFGHAN (Detail), page 127

PORTFOLIO of DESIGNS

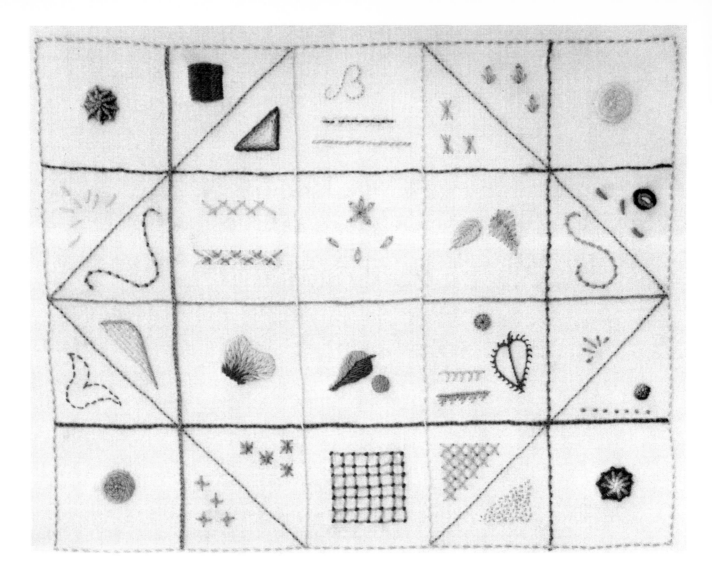

Beginner Stitch Sampler

MATERIALS

Linen, 20 x 18 inches

Crewel yarn, 3 ply. Choose an attractive palette of about fifteen colors. About 1 yard of each color should be sufficient. Be sure to include four shades of one of the colors to be used for Long and Short, Split Stitch and the Whipped Spider Web.

FINISHED SIZE

13 x 16 inches

NOTE

Separate the yarn and work all stitches with a single ply.

INSTRUCTIONS

It is essential that a piece like this be cut perfectly straight and best if the line stitches are worked along a thread of the fabric to insure that the block outlines are straight. To make certain the fabric is cut straight, pull a thread and cut along the line left by the missing thread.

Following the chart, lay out 3-inch squares on the linen. This can be done most accurately by placing small basting stitches with colored thread along a thread of the fabric. If you prefer, mark the lines lightly with a fine-point waterproof pen. Trace around a coin to make circles in the four corner squares; draw simple leaf and flower petal outlines, scrolls, and small circles where needed. Do not worry if your shapes are not exactly like the ones on the chart. Other stitches shown are to be worked freehand, without guide lines but following the written instructions for the blocks.

The chart indicates the layout for the sampler as it appears in the photograph, but feel free to place your stitches differently if you wish. To make the diagrammed sampler easier to read, printed stitch names have been used. Label yours with the fine-tipped waterproof pen so you will be able easily to identify the stitches later. You will find it easier to write in the names with the fabric stretched in the hoop or frame.

When you begin working, follow the written instructions here and turn back to the Stitch Dictionary for the detailed directions for making each stitch. Work the entire sampler with a single ply of the crewel yarn.

Work the stitches outlining the blocks first. These stitches have numbers to indicate their working order in brackets following the stitch names. Start working with the horizontal line marked Split Stitch [1]. Work it in medium blue. Next work the horizontal labeled Outline Stitch [2] in a pale beige. Chain Stitch [3] is medium green. The vertical Chain [4] is pale beige. Outline [5] is yellow. Whipped Running [6] is worked with a row of pale pink Running Stitches whipped with yellow. The Coral Stitch [7] vertical line is medium green.

Outline the entire rectangle with Whipped Running [8]. The Running Stitch for this row is pink, the Whipping Stitch lavender. Finally, work the diagonal lines in Back [9] in medium blue.

You may work the stitches in the blocks in any order pleasing and convenient to you. For instance, you may find that with a 12-inch hoop, blocks 1, 2, 3, 8, 9, and 10 are placed so they can be worked without moving the hoop. It makes sense to work all of them rather than trying to adhere to the numerical order, but for your convenience, the stitches used in the numbered blocks are listed in that order with hints about the colors used in the original and any working tips that will help you.

1. *Whipped Spider Web.* Pale blue. Work as per stitch directions, whipping the spokes until the web is raised above the surface of the linen.

2. *Roumanian Couching.* Medium green. Work a square about ¾ inch x ¾ inch, placing stitches close together to cover the fabric.

3. *Split Stitch.* Four shades of orange red. Work a little triangle that roughly echoes the outline of the space. Work with the four shades of red, beginning with the deepest tone at the outside edge and ending with the palest tone in the center. Leave the small space in the middle unworked.

4. *Back Stitch.* Pink, yellow, and pale blue. Draw one of your initials just above the middle of this square and work it in pale pink Back Stitch. Below the initial work a 1½-inch line of blue Back Stitch; interlace it with yellow. Work another blue line 2 inches long about ½ inch below the one just completed. Whip this one with yellow.

5. *Sheaf.* Pale green. Work three groups of stitches, placing them as shown on the chart.

6. *Tête de Boeuf.* Medium pink. Place three stitches as shown on the chart.

7. *Woven Spider Web.* Yellow. Work as directed, weaving round and round until the circle is raised nicely.

8. *Straight Stitch.* Yellow. Practice the long Straight Stitches, placing them as shown on the chart or at random, filling up the triangle.

9. *Couching.* Pink laid thread with medium blue tie-down stitches. Hold pink thread in place along the curved line and make small slanted blue stitches to hold it.

10. *Herringbone.* Green, yellow, aqua. Work top line of stitches ½-inch wide in green single Herringbone. Work another row about ¾ inch below, using yellow and aqua to work the double version of the stitch.

11. *Lazy Daisy.* Pale blue. Make a little flower shape with five stitches at the top center of the square. Scatter three single detached stitches below the flower.

12. *Fishbone.* Yellow and pale green. Work the yellow leaf in the closed version of the stitch to create a solid leaf, the pale green one open for a lacy stitch.

13. *Coral.* Rose. Work the scroll shape, placing the knots about ¼ inch apart.

14. *Bullion.* Two shades of orange red, and yellow. Work the oval flower shape by overlapping the stitches and wrapping the yarn around the needle so the stitches curve as in the stitch instructions. Make the center stitch yellow. Surround this with three of medium orange red. Make the outside stitches in the darkest shade of orange red. Scatter three single stitches below the flower.

15. *Running Stitch.* Medium blue. Outline the motif in fairly small Running Stitches so they fit neatly around the curves.

16. *Running Stitch.* Pink and blue. Work tiny pink Running Stitches in parallel rows beginning with the long side of the motif. Finish the curved edge with a line of Outline Stitch in blue.

17. *Long and Short.* Four shades of pink. Start working the flower petal at the outside edge with the palest shade of pink. Work toward the center, gradually shading to the deepest tone.

18. *Satin Stitch.* Orange and two shades of green. Use the orange for the small circle. Work a row of Split Stitch around the outline of the circle, then work the Satin Stitch. Outline the leaf sections with Split Stitch. Work one section in pale green, the other in medium green. Work the Satin Stitch so the stitches slant out from the center vein at an attractive angle.

19. *Buttonhole.* Dark blue, lavender, and pale rose. Work the leaf shape in dark blue with the stitches turned outward to give the spiked effect. The vein is Outline Stitch. The small lavender circle should be worked with all stitches intersecting in the center hole to create the wheel effect. Work a line about 1-inch long in the simplest Buttonhole with regular spacing in green. About ½ inch below that, work a slightly longer row, practicing one of the other versions of Buttonhole, using the rose yarn.

20. *French Knot on a Long Stem.* Medium orange red. Work as directed, placing five stitches as shown on the chart.

21. *French Knot.* Three shades of orange red. Using the next to darkest shade, work a row of evenly spaced stitches about ½ inch from the bottom line of the triangle. Work a small circle, using closely spaced knots, and work in shading, using the reds from the darkest one at the lower right edge to the lightest at the top.

22. *Woven Spider Web.* Pale green. Work as directed, weaving round and round to make a nicely raised circle.

23. *Four-Legged Knot.* Orange. Place four stitches as shown on the chart.

24. *Star.* Aqua. Work as per stitch instructions, placing four stitches as shown on the chart.

25. *Trellis Couching.* Aqua and red. Lay out a square about ½ inch smaller on all sides than the outlined block. Use the aqua for the laid threads. Make little slanted red stitches for the tie-downs.

26. *Cross Stitch.* Pale blue. There are five rows of crosses. The top one is five stitches wide, and each successive row is one stitch shorter which makes the triangle shape of the worked area. Make the arms of the crosses about ¼ inch long.

27. *Seeding.* Lavender. Place the stitches at random, filling a triangular space.

28. *Whipped Spider Web.* Four shades of orange red. Work as directed but use four shades of red for the whipping thread so the web is the palest shade at the center and works out to the darkest at the outside.

If you wish, eliminate the Spider Web and use this block for your name and the date the sampler was finished.

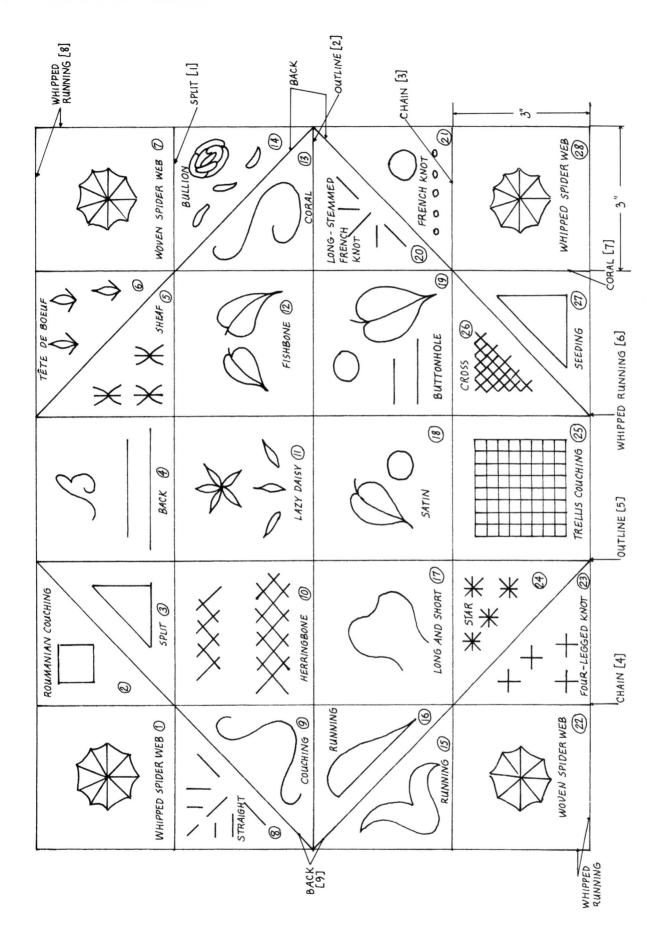

BEGINNER STITCH SAMPLER

55

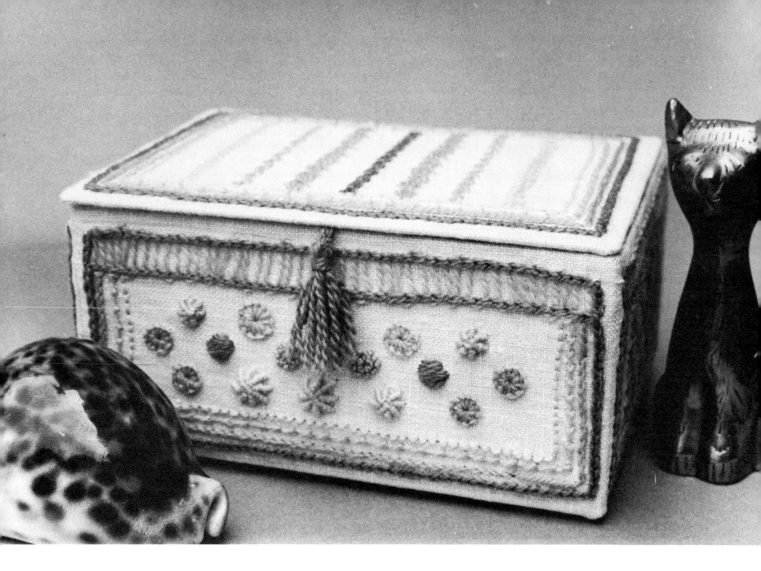

Embroidered Box

Each of the four sides and the top of this little box is a small stitch sampler worked in four muted shades of beige. Eighteen stitches create texture and simple design which transform an ordinary cardboard box into a decorative accessory.

This was a department store gift box 6¼ inches x 4½ inches x 3 inches, and the instructions that follow are for that size, but a glance at the charts for the box will make it apparent that the design can be enlarged or reduced easily. Originally the box top had sides that fit down over the edges of the lower section. These were cut off and replaced with a fabric hinge, a more practical construction when fabric covering is used.

MATERIALS
Linen, ¼ yard
Contrasting lining fabric, ¼ yard
Crewel yarn, 6 yards each: 015, Antique White; 496, Parchment; 492, Dust; 466, Light Brown
Box, 6¼ x 4½ x 3 inches
Thick white craft glue

NOTE
Separate the yarn and use a single ply for all stitches.

56

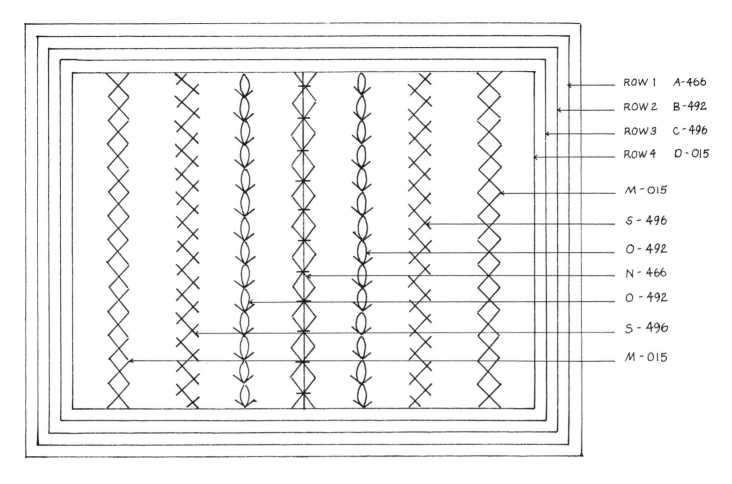

	ROW 1	A-466
	ROW 2	B-492
	ROW 3	C-496
	ROW 4	D-015
	M-015	
	S-496	
	O-492	
	N-466	
	O-492	
	S-496	
	M-015	

EMBROIDERED BOX   Top

STITCHES

A- Chain
B- Outline
C- Coral
D- Back
E- Trellis Couching
F- Lazy Daisy
G- Upright Cross
H- Whipped Spider Web
J- Buttonhole
K- French Knot
L- Satin Stitch
M- Cross
N- Sheaf
O- Tête de Boeuf
P- Four-Legged Knot
Q- Double Cross
R- Long-Stemmed French Knot
S- Herringbone

COLORS

015- Antique White
496- Parchment
492- Dust
466- Light Brown

INSTRUCTIONS

Cut one piece of linen 28 inches x 6 inches for the body of the box. Cut another 7 inches x 9 inches for the top.

With the transfer pencil, trace all five panels. Center the design for the top of the box on the 7 x 9 inch piece of linen and transfer it to the fabric. Transfer the side and end panel designs to the long strip, placing the panels end to end and matching the outlined edges of the charts. Let end outlines fall on top of adjoining outlines. Place end panel #1 at left side of the linen strip, followed by side panel #1; end panel #2 and side panel #2 in order. Center the panels so that there is an equal amount of linen border at top and bottom and at both ends.

Top. Start with Row 1 which is Chain Stitch outlining the rectangle. Follow with Rows 2, 3, and 4, using the colors indicated. Next work the vertical stripes, following the chart for color and stitches to be used.

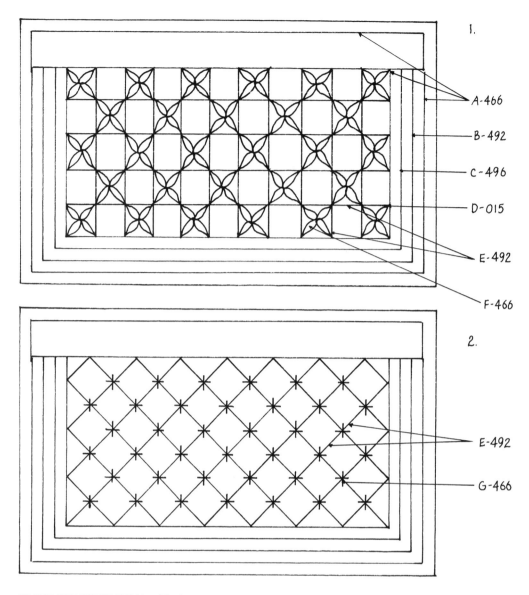

1.

A-466
B-492
C-496
D-015
E-492
F-466

2.

E-492
G-466

EMBROIDERED BOX   End Panels

End Panel #1. Begin with the four rows of stitching outlining the bottom and side edges of the panel. Add the two rows of Chain Stitch across the top. With 015, weave between the rows of Chain to form the row of vertical threads connecting the two rows. (See Interlaced Chain in Stitch Dictionary, but work over the two rows instead of only one as shown in the stitch instructions. To do this, bring the needle up at the top of one row, slide the needle under the first Chain Stitch and across to the other row. Without piercing the fabric, slide the needle under the first Chain Stitch. Turn the needle and slide under the next stitch. Go back across to the op-posite row and slide under the next of the Chain Stitches. Continue working back and forth to the end of the row.)

Following the instructions for Trellis Couching, lay out the square pattern shown on the chart. To tie down the laid threads, make four Lazy Daisy Stitches which intersect in the center of the alternate squares. Use the tacking stitch of the Lazy Daisy to tie down the laid threads, noting that these tie-down stitches are double where flower squares are adjoining.

Side Panel #1. Work border and top rows as in previous section. Fill circular motifs with the stitches and colors shown on the chart. Whip

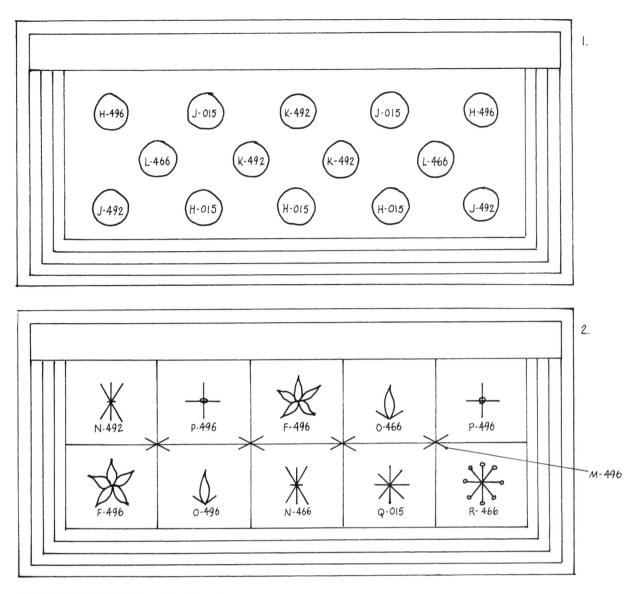

EMBROIDERED BOX   Side Panels

Spider Webs heavily to make them nice and high.

End Panel #2. Work border and top rows as in the previous sections. Lay diagonal Trellis Couching threads along the stamped lines. Work upright Cross Stitches over intersections of threads as in illustration on chart.

Side Panel #2. Work border and top rows as for other pieces. Lay yarn along stamped lines to form large squares. Tie down at intersections with Cross Stitch. Work the individual stitches, placing them in the centers of the squares and using the colors indicated on the chart.

Finishing. Block the embroidery. Glue the pieces to the box, working first on the top. Center the piece on the cardboard, turn three edges to the underside, and glue in place. Glue the fourth long side to the outside lower body of the box to form a hinge. Glue side and end panel strip to box, turning raw edges to inside at top and pulling raw edges to underside at bottom. Glue lining fabric to inside to cover all raw edges. Glue a rectangle of lining fabric on bottom, again to cover all raw edges.

Make a small tassel. Tuck ends of tassel under the lining of top of box and glue it in place.

Oval Picture

This graceful flower spray is worked in seven of the most valuable crewel stitches and is a charming introduction to embroidery with wool. The soft sea foam blues, pale golds and accents of rust are lovely, but even a beginner should not hesitate to take a cue from another piece and apply other colors if they are more appealing. Bright colors or a monochromatic plan would both be attractive and would produce a very different effect.

MATERIALS
Linen, 12 x 14 inches
Crewel yarn: 468, Yellow White, 2 yards; 438, Buttercup, 1 yard; 453, Warm Sands, 2 yards; R78, Pink Blush, 2 yards; 255*, Rose, 2 yards; 354, Light Foam, 2 yards; 352, Foam, 3 yards; 367, Sea Green, 4 yards.
Oval or rectangular frame, 8 x 10 inches

FINISHED SIZE
8 x 10 inches

NOTE
Separate the yarn and work all embroidery with a single ply.

INSTRUCTIONS
Trace the outline drawing and transfer it to linen following the instructions on page 13. The drawing is a mirror image of the photographed finished picture so that when the drawing is traced with transfer pencil and ironed on the linen, it will appear like the model.

Before beginning to work, read the Working Tips for basic embroidery instructions. See the Stitch Dictionary for directions for each stitch as it is needed.

Stretch the linen in a hoop or frame. Begin working on the Outline Stitch flower stems, using the colors noted on the chart. Next work the central flower, and then move on to other areas in any order desired.

Outline all Satin and Fishbone Stitch areas with fine Split Stitch before working the finishing stitches. This will pad those stitches and make them nicely raised.

Work French Knots as close together as possible to cover the linen completely.

When working the solid Outline Stitch leaves, work the outline of the shape, then work concentric rows inside, placing the rows as close as possible to fill the area completely.

Note that when motifs are to be worked with Trellis Couching, two numbers separated by a slashed line appear. The first number always indicates the color of the laid thread, the second the color of the tie-down thread. Finish the two steps of Couching in these areas before working the Outline around the motif to achieve a smooth edge.

Finish the embroidery, block, and frame as directed in those special chapters of the book devoted to those instructions.

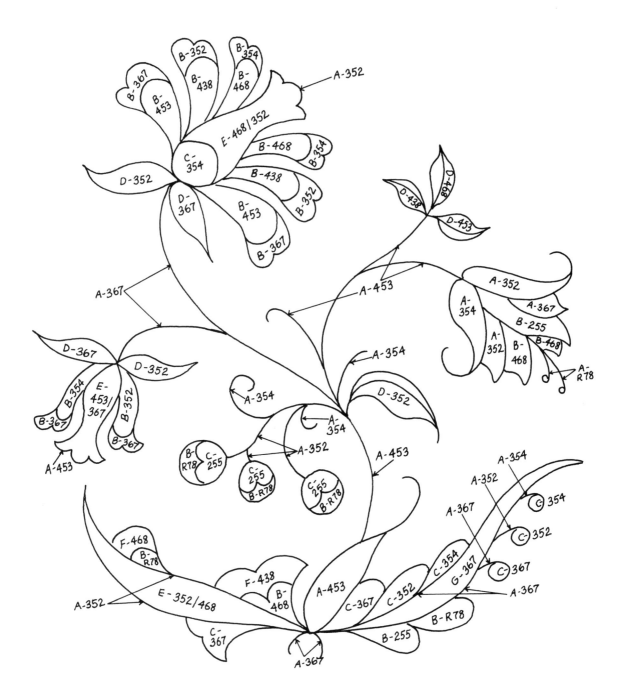

OVAL PICTURE

STITCHES

A- Outline
B- Satin
C- French Knot
D- Fishbone
E- Trellis Couching
F- Buttonhole
G- Seeding

COLORS

468- Yellow White
438- Buttercup
453- Warm Sands
R78- Pink Blush
255*- Rose
354- Light Foam
352- Foam
367- Sea Green

Two Pincushions

A pretty pincushion is a feminine touch on the dressing table or useful as a sewing accessory, but it also makes a lovely special gift and is a great way to use up scraps of fabric and yarn. These two pincushions have been finished with lace ruffles but can be tailored with a cord trim for a different look. They would also be a suitable beginner project as they use basic stitches and are small enough to finish quickly.

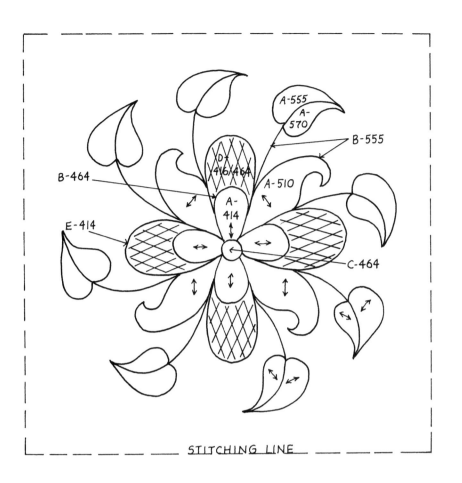

STITCHING LINE

COLORS

464- Orange Ice
416- Light Rust
414- Rust
570- Celery Leaf
555- Green Giant
510- Medium Green

STITCHES

A- Satin
B- Outline
C- French Knot
D- Trellis Couching
E- Chain

Lace-edged Square Pincushion

MATERIALS
    Cream colored linen, 8 x 16 inches
    Small amount of polyester filler
    Cotton lace, 1½ inches wide, 1 yard
    Crewel yarn: 464, Orange Ice, 1 yard; 416,
        Light Rust, 1 yard; 414, Rust, 2 yards; 570,
        Celery Leaf, 3 yards; 555, Green Giant, 3
        yards; 510, Medium Green, 2 yards

FINISHED SIZE
    4¼ x 4¼ inches excluding the lace

NOTE
    Separate the yarn and embroider with a single
ply.

INSTRUCTIONS
    The arrows on the chart show the direction of
the slant of the Satin Stitch areas. In the leaves
that are to be worked in Trellis Couching, lay
the diagonal threads with 416 and tie down with
464. Cluster French Knots close in center to
cover linen completely.
    Block embroidery. Trim, leaving ½ inch be-
yond stitching line. Cut backing to match. Construct like a small pillow, inserting gathered lace
in the seam. Stuff and close seam.

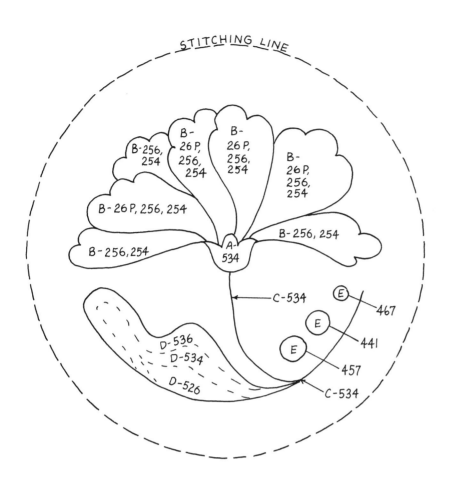

STITCHING LINE

COLORS

26P- Cloud Pink
256- Snow Petal
254- Dusty Pink
536- Mint Julep
534- Light Green
526- Green
467- Light Medium Yellow
441- Medium Yellow
457- Canary Yellow

STITCHES

A- Satin
B- Long and Short
C- Coral
D- French Knot
E- Buttonhole

Lace-edged Round Pincushion

MATERIALS

Cream colored linen, 8 x 16 inches
Polyester filler, small amount
Cotton lace, 2 inches wide, 1 yard
Crewel yarn, about 1 yard each of the following: 26P, Cloud Pink; 256, Snow Petal; 254, Dusty Pink; 536, Mint Julep; 534, Light Green; 526, Green; 467, Light Medium Yellow; 441, Medium Yellow; 457, Canary Yellow

FINISHED SIZE

4¼ inches diameter without lace

NOTE

Work all embroidery with a single-ply yarn.

INSTRUCTIONS

Trace the design and transfer it to the linen, spacing it so there will be room to cut a piece the same size for the back.

First work the three flower petals that use just two shades of pink. Keep the darkest value at the base and lower edges of the petals. When working the remaining petals, keep the darkest shade at the base and to the center so the lighter shades can delineate the edges and separate them.

Complete the embroidery. Block and trim, leaving a ½-inch border beyond the stitching line. Cut back to match. Gather lace and sew it into the seam joining front to back. Turn right side out. Stuff and close seam.

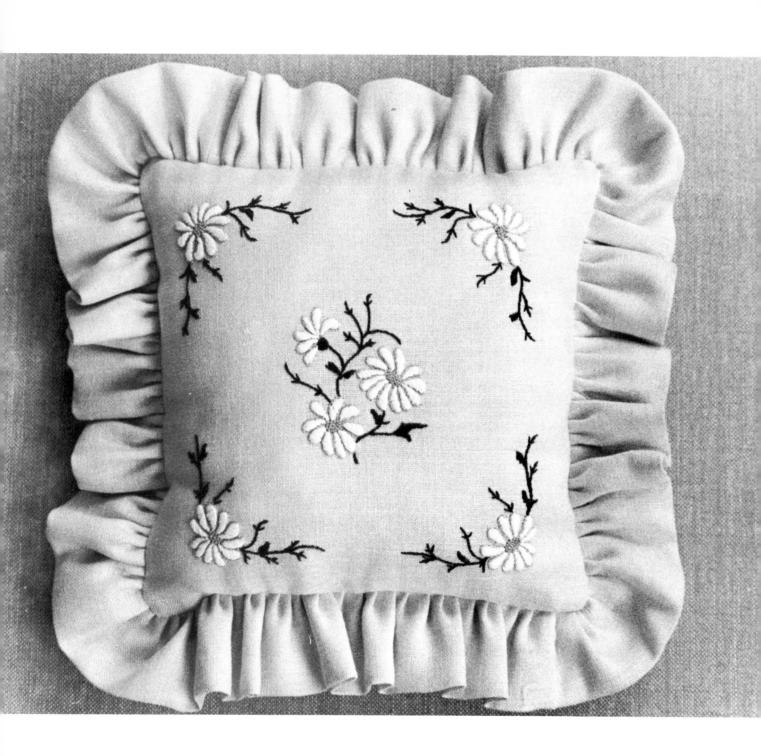

Daisies, everyone's favorite flower, decorate this dainty yellow linen confection and the lace-trimmed ring bearer's pillow on page 71. The latter bears the names of the bride and groom and the date of the wedding; the central spray of flowers was eliminated to make room for the inscription, bow, and the words "With this ring . . ."

Both pillows are small and dainty. The yellow one measures 11 inches x 11 inches including the 2-inch ruffle; the bridal pillow is 10 inches x 10 inches including the gathered 2½-inch-wide lace.

Although crewel is properly worked only with a wool thread, the yellow pillow has been embroidered with six-strand cotton floss to illustrate the difference this kind of thread makes in a design. Substitute wool in similar colors if you wish. The wedding pillow is shown worked in wool. This one will be treasured and loved by the bride long after the wedding day.

Daisy Pillow

MATERIALS
Yellow linen, ¾ yard
DMC Embroidery floss, 1 skein each: White; 367, Dark Green; 813, Pale Blue; 725, Orange

FINISHED SIZE
11 x 11 inches including ruffle

NOTE
Work all stitches with three strands of embroidery floss except for the blue outlines around the daisy petals. These should be worked with a single strand.

INSTRUCTIONS
Fold tracing paper in half vertically. Open flat and place over chart, matching the fold line to the dotted center line on the chart. Trace. Copy the stitching lines as a series of dots to be used as a guide when constructing the pillow.

Fold the tracing paper on the fold line again, and trace the corner daisies again to complete the design. Cut two 13-inch squares from the linen. Center the design on one and transfer it.

Embroider, using the portion of the chart marked for embroidery floss for reference. All daisies are to be white Satin Stitch, outlined with a single strand of blue. Flower centers are clustered French Knots while stems are dark green Outline and leaves are Satin Stitch.

Using the remaining fabric to make a ruffle, construct the pillow.

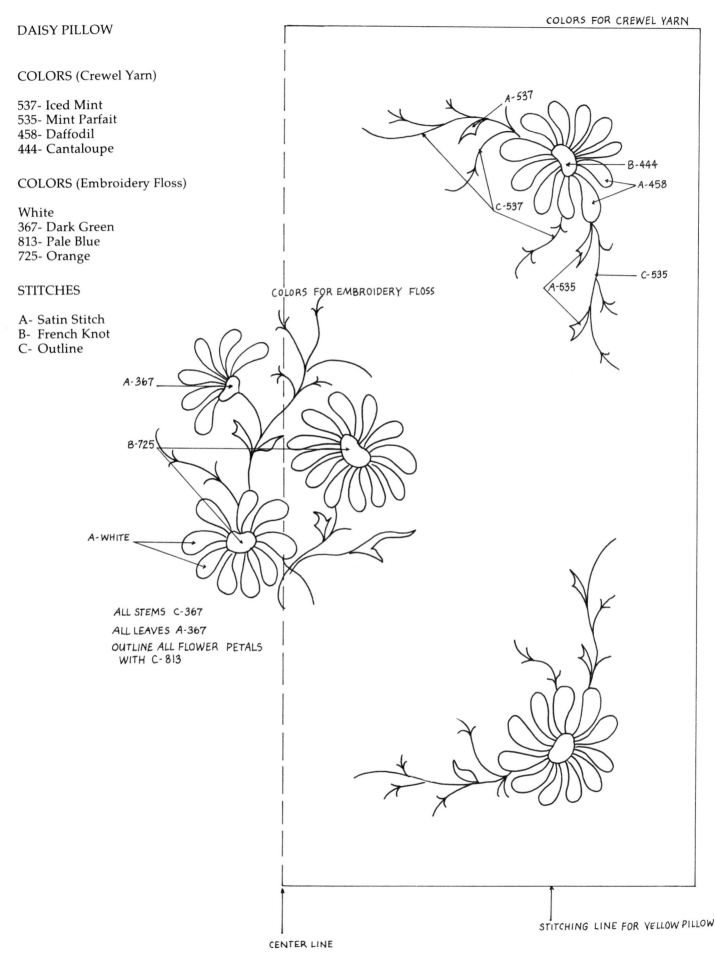

DAISY PILLOW

COLORS (Crewel Yarn)

537- Iced Mint
535- Mint Parfait
458- Daffodil
444- Cantaloupe

COLORS (Embroidery Floss)

White
367- Dark Green
813- Pale Blue
725- Orange

STITCHES

A- Satin Stitch
B- French Knot
C- Outline

COLORS FOR CREWEL YARN

A-537

B-444

A-458

C-537

C-535

A-535

COLORS FOR EMBROIDERY FLOSS

A-367

B-725

A-WHITE

ALL STEMS C-367

ALL LEAVES A-367

OUTLINE ALL FLOWER PETALS
  WITH C-813

STITCHING LINE FOR YELLOW PILLOW

CENTER LINE

70

Bridal Pillow

MATERIALS
White linen, ½ yard
Crewel yarn: 458, Daffodil, 3 yards; 537, Iced Mint, 1 yard; 535, Mint Parfait, 2 yards; 444, Cantaloupe, 1 yard; B42, Whisper Blue, 2 yards
White satin ribbon, 3/16 inch wide, 2 yards
White lace, 2½ inches wide, 1¾ yards

FINISHED SIZE
10 x 10 inches

NOTE
Separate the yarn and work all stitches with a single strand.

INSTRUCTIONS
Fold tracing paper and copy the design as in the instructions for the yellow pillow, omitting the center spray of flowers and using the stitching line as the cutting line since this pillow is to be smaller. Measure down from the top cutting line, about 2 inches, and draw a light line. In script write "With this ring . . ." Write the names of the bride and groom 2 inches below center of pillow and below that, the date of the wedding.

Cut two 12-inch squares of linen. Center the tracing on one and transfer the design. Embroider, following the chart marked for crewel yarn. Use the pale blue (B42) yarn to embroider the inscription with small Back Stitches.

Block. Construct pillow. Make a bow with the ribbon and attach it to the center of the pillow. The rings are fastened to the ends of the ribbons for the ceremony.

Justin and Kirsten

In their pretty yellow frames, Justin and Kirsten are a pair of gay pastel pictures with unusual embroidered mats. They would be cute in a child's room or anywhere a bit of whimsey is needed.

Kirsten is dressed in her Sunday best: straw hat with blue streamers, shiny black Mary Janes, and bow-tied apron over her sunny yellow dress. Her hair is a mass of golden brown waves worked in Couching. Her bouquet is worked entirely in Bullion Stitch—pink and blue flowers with yellow centers and green leaves.

Justin has just changed into clean jeans and yellow sweater to go play with his new bow and arrow. The jeans are detailed with pockets and jaunty seams. His hair is a tangle of curls worked in Bullion Knots.

Outline details of both pictures—sweater and jeans, dress and bows—are worked with two strands of cotton embroidery floss, both for the effect of the contrasting material and for the thinner line possible. The garland of flowers around the oval frame is alternating pink and blue Bullion Knot buds with a pair of leaves between each pair of flowers. The embroidered mat has evenly spaced blue Bullion Stitch flowers with yellow flowers.

KIRSTEN

MATERIALS

Linen, two pieces 12 x 14 inches

Crewel yarn: 865, Powder Pink, 14 yards; 853,
Flesh, 6 yards; 456, Baby Yellow, 6 yards;
537, Iced Mint, 8 yards; 781* Baby Blue, 14
yards; 455, Honey, 1 yard; 050, Black, 1
yard; 005, White 2 yards; 445, Antique
Gold, 3 yards.

Cotton Embroidery floss: Pale Blue, 1 yard;
Pale Yellow, 2 yards

Picture frames, two, 8 x 10 inches

FINISHED SIZE

8 x 10 inches

NOTE

Separate the crewel yarn and work all embroidery stitches with a single ply. Work all embroidery floss details with two strands.

Kirsten

INSTRUCTIONS

Fold tracing paper into quarters. Open flat. Match fold lines to dotted lines on chart. Trace figure, oval, and the quarter of mat shown. Fold the paper again on the fold lines and trace the quarter mat three times to complete. Transfer to linen.

Embroider, following the chart and referring to the photograph for help with details. The arrows on the chart indicate the slant of the stitches.

Work the Chain Stitch crown of hat in a curved line, following the outline of the top. Slant Satin Stitch of bows in different directions to differentiate the areas from one another. Outline the bow and hatband in Outline Stitch with two strands of pale blue embroidery floss.

Lay couching threads for hair and hat brim, following the outline of the shapes. Work back and forth inside the hairline, placing rows close together and tying often to create curves that look like curls.

The apron is vertical rows of Outline Stitch with a blue outline and fold details. Work apron bow as for hat ribbon and outline it also with blue embroidery floss. Work Satin Stitch skirt; then with two strands of yellow floss, work Trellis Couching on top. Also outline the hemline with embroidery floss.

The bouquet should be tightly packed pink and blue rosebuds. To make each: make two Bullion Stitch knots side by side with ends touching as shown on the chart. Center with a yellow French Knot. Fill entire bouquet area with these alternating pink and blue rosebuds, interspersing them with a few green Bullion leaves.

On each dot on the embroidered mat, make a Bullion flower like the one shown on the chart: one yellow stitch with a blue one on either side and ends touching.

Over the oval picture outline, work a garland of Bullion rosebuds like those shown at the bottom of the oval. These flowers consist of a yellow center knot with three overlapping Bullion Stitches forming the flower. Alternate one pink flower with one blue one around the entire oval. Place two green Bullion Knot leaves between each pair of flowers, slanting the leaves slightly.

Block and frame as shown.

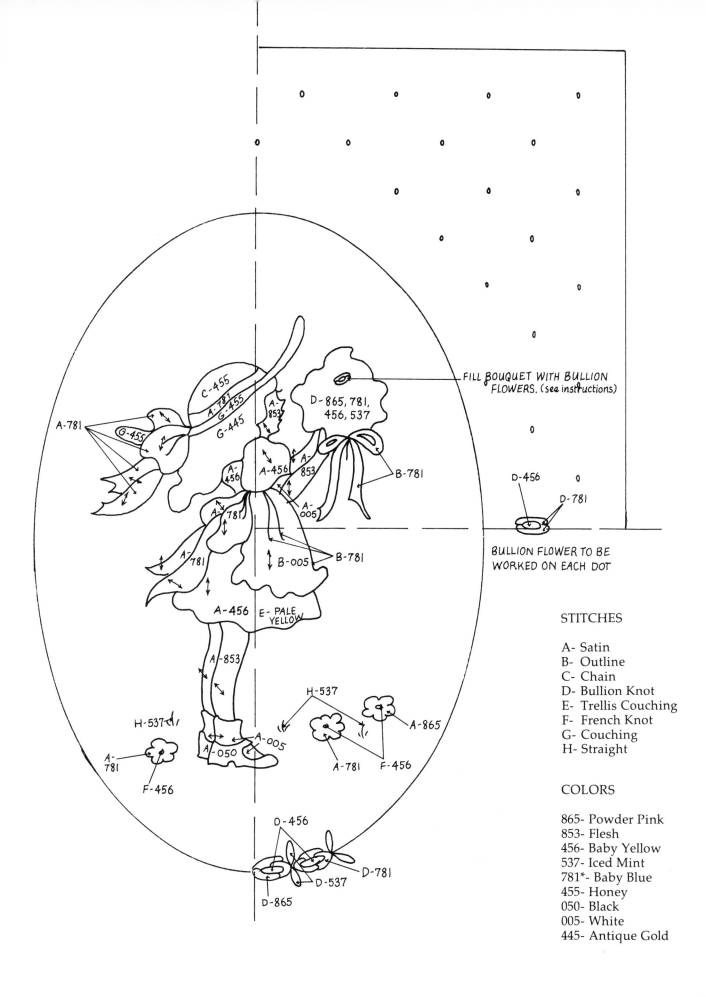

FILL BOUQUET WITH BULLION FLOWERS. (see instructions)

BULLION FLOWER TO BE WORKED ON EACH DOT

C-455
A-781
G-455
G-445

A-781

G-455

A-781

A-853

A-456

A-456

A-781

A-005

A-853

D-865, 781, 456, 537

B-781

B-781

B-005

A-456

E- PALE YELLOW

H-537

A-865

H-537

A-781

F-456

H-537

A-781

F-456

A-005

A-050

D-456

D-781

D-456

D-781

D-537

D-865

STITCHES

A- Satin
B- Outline
C- Chain
D- Bullion Knot
E- Trellis Couching
F- French Knot
G- Couching
H- Straight

COLORS

865- Powder Pink
853- Flesh
456- Baby Yellow
537- Iced Mint
781*- Baby Blue
455- Honey
050- Black
005- White
445- Antique Gold

75

JUSTIN (Detail)

Justin

Trace, following the mat drawing and the instructions as for Kirsten. Work the Satin Stitch areas, slanting in the directions shown by the arrows. With two strands of pale yellow embroidery floss, work an Outline Stitch around all details of the sweater, including collar, cuffs, sleeves, waistband, and outside edges. Outline the jeans in the same manner, adding pocket and seam detail with two strands of pale blue embroidery floss.

Work bow in blue wool Outline Stitch; then with yellow embroidery floss, work an Outline Stitch on each side of the blue row. The arrow head is green Satin Stitch with three Straight Stitches of yellow floss to outline it.

Fill hair section with Bullion Knots, wrapping the needle enough to make the knots curve. Try to place the knots in wavy lines so they look like curls.

Embroider the oval garland and the mat as in the instructions for the little girl. Block and frame.

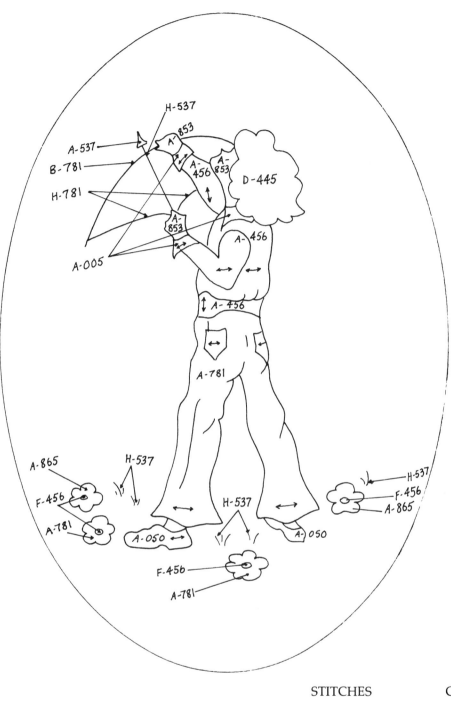

STITCHES

A- Satin
B- Outline
C- Chain
D- Bullion Knot
E- Trellis Couching
F- French Knot
G- Couching
H- Straight

COLORS

865- Powder Pink
853- Flesh
456- Baby Yellow
537- Iced Mint
781*- Baby Blue
455- Honey
050- Black
005- White
445- Antique Gold

77

Modern Jacobean Pillow

Fanciful Jacobean flowers that Mother Nature would never recognize adapt well to crewel embroidery. Colonial ladies who did not have access to design books drew flowers like this from memory to decorate their household furnishings, and the pieces remaining show so many of these flowers that many people refer to them as crewel flowers. The combination of Jacobean flowers and completely modern colors makes this a pillow that will be equally at home in either a traditional or a contemporary setting.

MATERIALS
Cream colored linen, ½ yard
Crewel yarn: 565, Yellow Green, 3 yards; 570, Celery Leaf, 2 yards; 555, Green Giant, 6 yards; 510, Medium Green, 5 yards; 395, Light Blue, 2 yards; 386, Blue Balloon, 2 yards; 385, French Blue, 2 yards; 467, Light Medium Yellow, 2 yards; 457, Canary Yellow, 3 yards; 447, Mustard, 4 yards; 427, Medium Gold, 3 yards; 831, Pale Pink, 5 yards; 281, Antique Pink, 3 yards; 234 Toasty Pink, 4 yards

FINISHED SIZE
14 x 14 inches

NOTE
Separate the yarn and use a single ply for all stitches.

INSTRUCTIONS
The design has been divided into two sections. Draw a vertical line about 2 inches to the right of the center of the tracing paper. Line this line up with the dashed line on the charts and trace the design, using the overlapping portions of design as well as the lines to insure proper alignment of the two sections.

Trace the design and transfer it to an 18-inch square of the linen. Embroider, following the chart for stitches and color placement.

The leaves under the blue flower are marked: D–510, 555, 570, 565. This means that they are to be worked in Split Stitch, beginning at the outside edge with one row of the darkest green (510), followed by one row of 555, then one of 570, then 565. There will be a small space remaining, and this should be filled with 565. Work the rows, following the outline of the leaf. The vein should be 510. Split Stitch areas on the gold flower and on the fan-shaped leaf at the bottom center are to be worked in the same manner, with the colors noted on the chart.

The strawberries are shaded Satin Stitch with a pale pink Trellis Couching laid on top. To work: first outline the berry with Split Stitch in 281. Then, beginning at the base, work Satin Stitch with 234 to cover a little less than one third the area. Change to 281 and work about one third more. Finish with 831. Lay couching thread of 831 as shown on the chart and tie down with the same color.

Slant the Roumanian Couching on the two large leaves below the gold flower in the direction of the arrows. Finish the leaves with an Outline Stitch along the outside edges and veins, in the colors noted on the chart.

Complete the embroidery. Cut a 15-inch square from the remaining fabric for pillow back. Trim front to 15 inches. Finish pillow, using self-cording made from the remaining fabric, or trim it with a contrasting color.

MODERN JACOBEAN PILLOW

Left Side

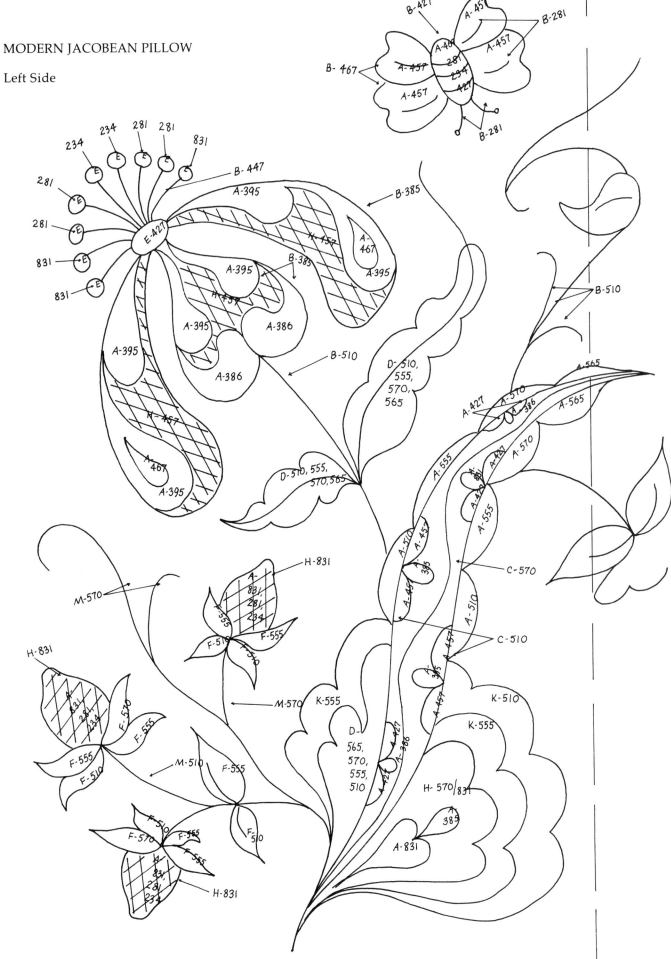

MODERN JACOBEAN PILLOW

Right Side

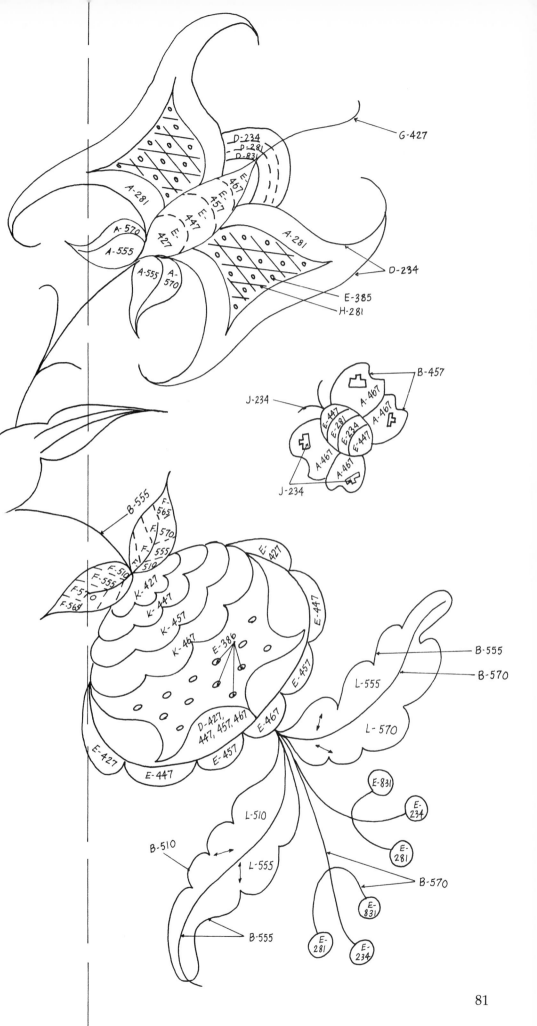

STITCHES

A- Satin
B- Outline
C- Chain
D- Split
E- French Knot
F- Fishbone
G- Back
H- Trellis Couching
J- Straight
K- Buttonhole
L- Roumanian Couching
M- Coral

COLORS

565- Yellow Green
570- Celery Leaf
555- Green Giant
510- Medium Green
395- Light Blue
386- Blue Balloon
385- French Blue
467- Light Medium Yellow
457- Canary Yellow
447- Mustard
427- Medium Gold
831- Pale Pink
281- Antique Pink
234- Toasty Pink

81

MODERN JACOBEAN PILLOW

Full View

This reduced version of the pattern shows what your tracing will look like when it's completed.

Jacobean Threesome

This grouping contains my favorite pieces in this book. I love the fanciful Jacobean flowers, pastel coloring, and the process of designing the flowers. I could happily fill my home with fabrics, wallpapers, embroidery, and collections of old pieces covered with these flowers. Have done a pretty good job of it, as a matter of fact, but I have restrained myself to keep it from becoming boring to others.

It is usually easy to find one picture or pillow that is perfect for a room, but seldom are two or three coordinating items available. To answer this need, here are a mini-panel, a bell pull, and a pillow with similar designs that are colored so

they can be used together. The bell pull and mini-panel have been embroidered in bright colors, but the pillow is shown in five natural shades. This shows the effect that a change of colors brings about. If you plan to work all three, use the colors of one on all of them. The stitching varies slightly from one piece to another for added variety. Working the same flower three times in the same stitches and colors becomes monotonous and is not as visually interesting.

Another pillow that has color and design close enough to be added to this collection is the Modern Jacobean on page 78.

Mini-Panel

MATERIALS

    Cream colored linen, 11 x 19 inches

    Backing fabric, ½ yard

    Polyester quilt filler, 7¼ x 14½ inches

    Crewel yarn: 570, Celery Leaf, 4 yards; 555, Green Giant, 4 yards; 510, Medium Green, 4 yards; 467, Light Medium Yellow, 4 yards; 441, Medium Yellow, 4 yards; 447, Mustard, 25 yards; 427, Medium Gold, 4 yards; 395, Light Blue, 3 yards; 385, French Blue, 3 yards; 334, Dark French Blue, 2 yards; 281, Antique Pink, 2 yards; 234, Toasty Pink, 3 yards

FINISHED SIZE

    7 x 14 inches

NOTE

    Separate the yarn and work all stitches with a single ply.

INSTRUCTIONS

    Fold tracing paper in half horizontally. Open flat; place fold line over the dotted line on the drawing for the top section of the panel. Trace.

    Move the tracing paper to the chart for the lower section. Line up the fold line with the dotted line on this chart. Make sure triangles and slanted lines match. Trace. Center the design on the linen and transfer it.

    Pad the gold outline frame with a row of Split Stitch on each edge. Begin and end all threads on the right side and work over them to add extra padding. This makes a lovely raised border.

    Work the Long and Short winged petals of the top flower, beginning with the deepest gold at the base and shading to the palest at the outside edges. Slant Satin Stitch for the small petals at the base of the flower in the direction of the arrows.

    The large leaf of the upper flower is marked: D–510, 555, 570, 467. Start working with 510 in

Split Stitch and outline the edge of the leaf. Next work one row of 555 just inside the outline. Continue with a row of 570, followed by a row of 467. There will be a small irregular space left unworked. The vein should be Chain Stitch in 510.

Slant the Satin Stitch in the lower flower and its leaves in the direction of the arrows on the chart. Lay the diagonal Couching threads inside the semicircular center sections of the flower; tie down with upright Straight Stitch; then place a long, gold Straight Stitch in each diamond as shown on the chart.

Follow the curving outline of the Split Stitch leaf to work the first row. Then work consecutive rows inside until the space is filled.

When embroidery is completed, block and finish, following the construction instructions for a bell pull on page 141. Use the polyester quilt filler as a padded interlining. The pictured panel is backed with very fine wale corduroy and has a corded trim of the same fabric.

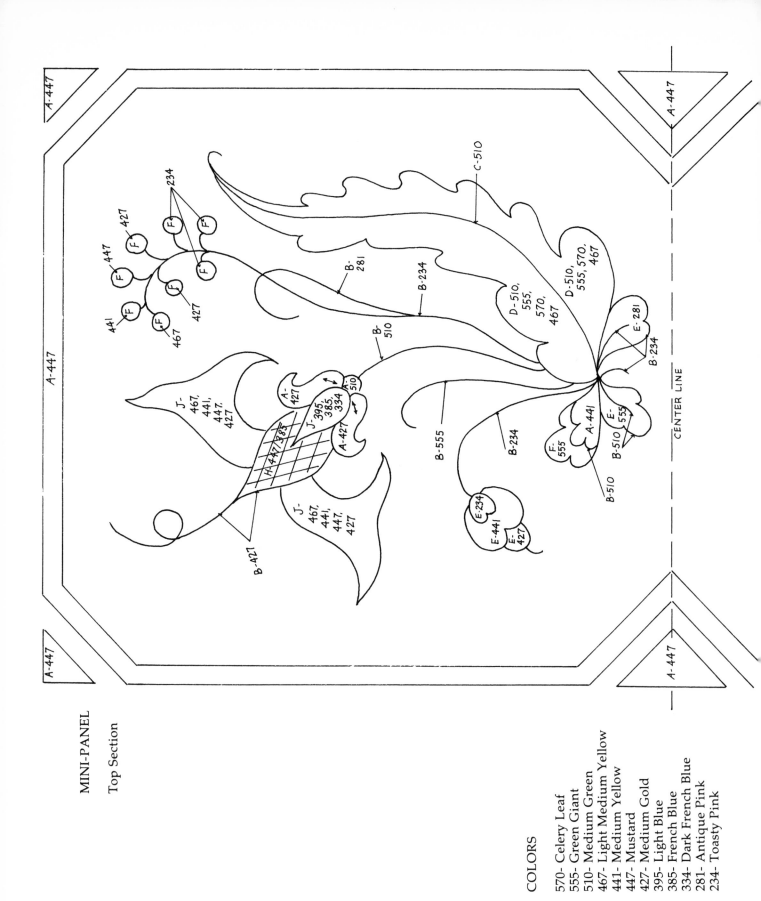

MINI-PANEL

Top Section

COLORS

570- Celery Leaf
555- Green Giant
510- Medium Green
467- Light Medium Yellow
441- Medium Yellow
447- Mustard
427- Medium Gold
395- Light Blue
385- French Blue
334- Dark French Blue
281- Antique Pink
234- Toasty Pink

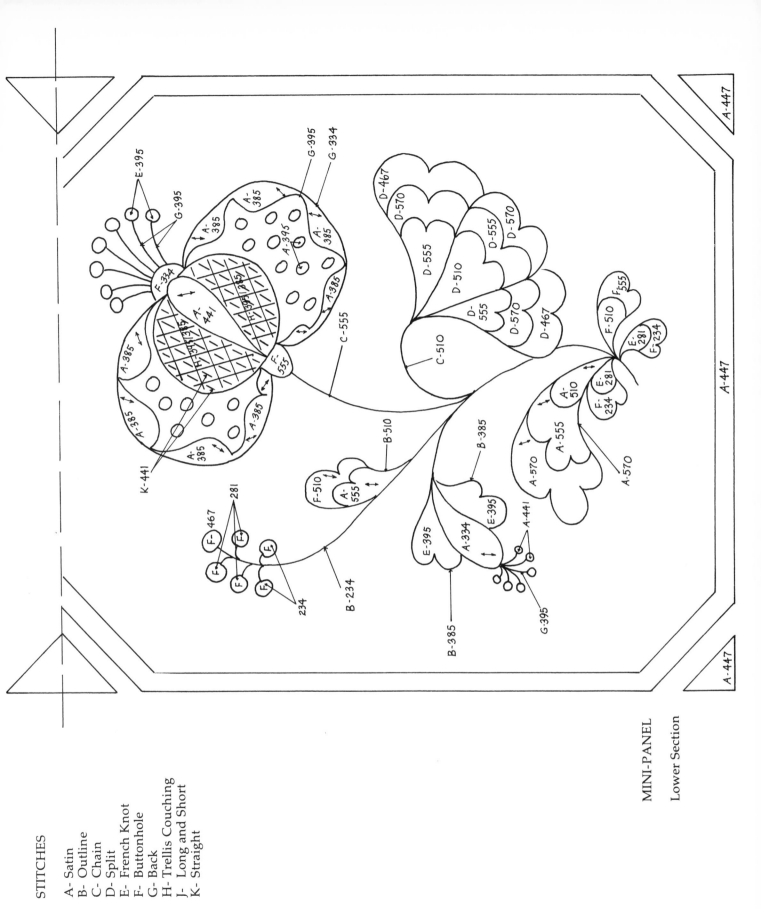

STITCHES

A- Satin
B- Outline
C- Chain
D- Split
E- French Knot
F- Buttonhole
G- Back
H- Trellis Couching
J- Long and Short
K- Straight

MINI-PANEL
Lower Section

87

Bell Pull

MATERIALS

    Cream colored linen, 8 x 30 inches
    Backing fabric, ½ yard
    Polyester quilt filler, 5½ x 26 inches
    Metal bell pull hardware as shown
    Crewel yarn: 447, Mustard, 30 yards; 6 yards
      each of the following: 831, Pale Pink; 281,
      Antique Pink; 234, Toasty Pink; 570, Celery
      Leaf; 555, Green Giant; 510, Medium
      Green; 467, Light Medium Yellow; 441, Me-
      dium Yellow; 395, Light Blue; 385, French
      Blue; 334, Dark French Blue

FINISHED SIZE

    5½ x 25½ inches

NOTE

    Embroider all stitches with a single ply of the
yarn.

INSTRUCTIONS

    About an inch from the left side of the tracing
paper, draw a vertical straight line. Match this
line to the left border line on all sections of the
drawing to be sure that the borders always
match. If your paper is not long enough to trace
all four sections in the position to be transferred, they may be traced separately and then
lined up on the linen. Just be careful to line
them up along a straight line and to match the
triangles where the sections join. The triangles
are shown on all sections as a guide to correct
placement.

    Center the design on the linen and transfer it.

Pad the gold outline frame with a row of Split Stitch on each edge. Begin and end all threads on the right side and work over them to add padding. This makes a lovely raised border. Since there is so much of this border, you may want to work small amounts of it at a time to keep it from being tiresome.

Flower #1. Work the center French Knot section, placing the stitches very close to completely cover the linen. Shade by using the blues shown inside the dotted lines. Outline this section with Split Stitch in 441.

The large blue winged petals are marked: D–395, 385, 334, denoting that they are to be worked in Split Stitch, beginning with 395 at the outside edges and shading to the darkest blue in the center. It will take two rows of each shade to fill the petals.

The small gold winged petals are to be worked in Long and Short, shading from the darkest gold at the inside to the lightest shade at the tips.

Slant the Roumanian Couching in the direction of the arrows on the leaf on which it is used. For the leaf that is to be worked in Trellis Couching, lay the 555 threads in the diagonal pattern, then tie them down with small Straight Stitches of 467. Outline the entire leaf with 555.

Arrows show direction of Satin Stitches. Finish other stitches, using the colors noted on the chart.

Flower #2. Work the Split Stitch leaves in the proper color, beginning at the outside edge and working concentric rows inside the outline until the leaf is completely filled.

Slant Satin Stitches in direction shown by the arrows. Lay 234 threads for Trellis Couching in the center section of the flower, then tie down with small Straight Stitches of 447. Outline the section with 234 Outline Stitch. Shade the three French Knot petals by working the shades of gold within the dotted lines. Start the Long and Short petals with the deepest gold at the inside and shade outward to the lightest gold at the edge.

Flower #3. Lay 831 threads for Trellis Couching in the center of the flower and tie down with 234. Also work Outline Stitch of 234 around the section. Use the deepest shade of pink at the base of the Long and Short petals and the next value at the edges. Finish the petals with Buttonhole in 831, as noted on the chart. As for other flowers, arrows denote slant of Satin Stitches. In the Trellis Couching for the long leaf, lay threads of 570 in the diamond pattern, then tie down with 385.

Flower #4. Outline the center with one row of French Knots in 447. Follow with a row of 441, then fill remainder of space with 467. Trellis Couching should be worked as in other flowers: lay threads of 395 and tie down with 334. Complete embroidery. Block and finish, following construction details on page 141. If a tassel like the one shown is desired, it will require an additional 25-yard skein of color 447. Instructions for making the tassel are on page 141.

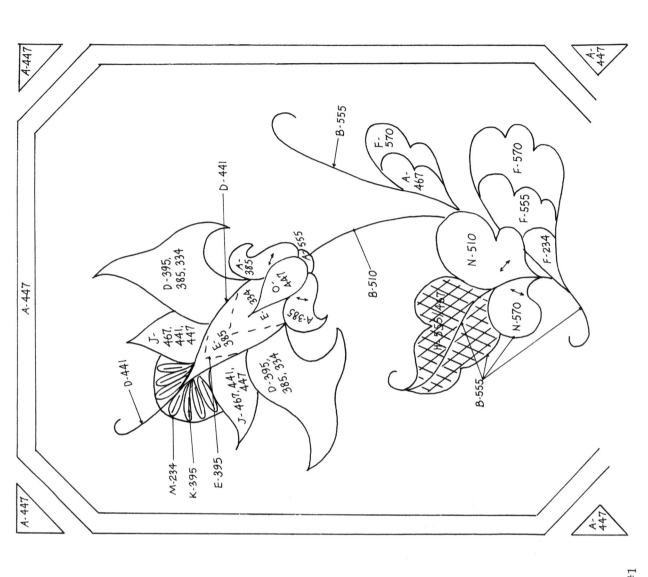

STITCHES

A- Satin
B- Outline
C- Chain
D- Split
E- French Knot
F- Buttonhole
G- Back
H- Trellis Couching
J- Long and Short
K- Straight
M- Lazy Daisy
N- Roumanian Couching
O- Fishbone
P- Coral

COLORS

831- Pale Pink
281- Antique Pink
234- Toasty Pink
570- Celery Leaf
555- Green Giant
510- Medium Green
467- Light Medium Yellow
441- Medium Yellow
447- Mustard
395- Light Blue
385- French Blue
334- Dark French Blue

BELL PULL   Flower #1

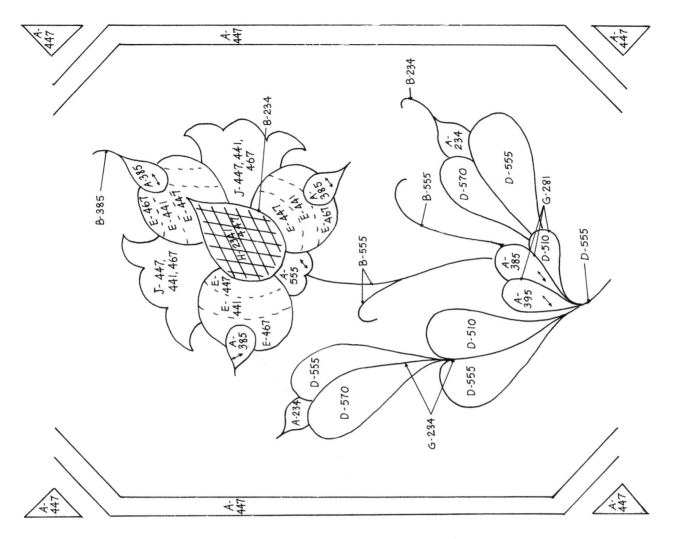

BELL PULL   Flower #2

91

STITCHES

A- Satin
B- Outline
C- Chain
D- Split
E- French Knot
F- Buttonhole
G- Back
H- Trellis Couching
J- Long and Short
K- Straight
M- Lazy Daisy
N- Roumanian Couching
O- Fishbone
P- Coral

COLORS

831- Pale Pink
281- Antique Pink
234- Toasty Pink
570- Celery Leaf
555- Green Giant
510- Medium Green
467- Light Medium Yellow
441- Medium Yellow
447- Mustard
395- Light Blue
385- French Blue
334- Dark French Blue

BELL PULL   Flower #3

92

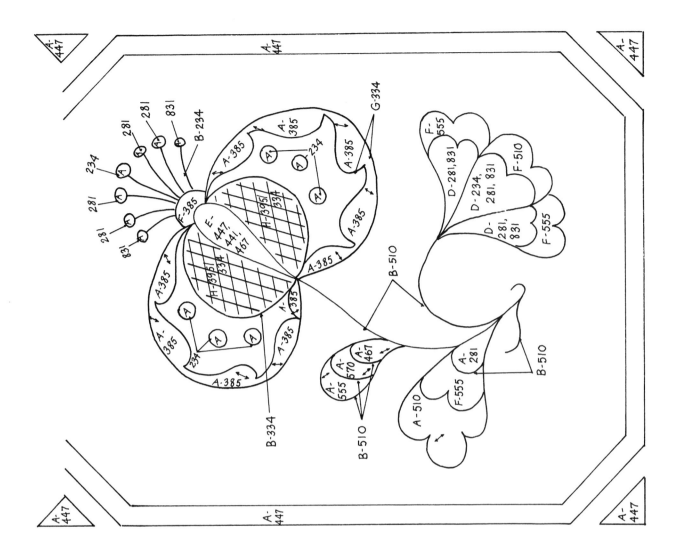

BELL PULL   Flower #4

Four Flowers Pillow

MATERIALS
  Cream colored linen, ½ yard
  Crewel yarn: 012, Ivory, 5 yards; 015, Antique
  White, 10 yards; 496, Parchment, 38 yards;
  492, Dust, 25 yards; 466, Light Brown, 12
  yards

FINISHED SIZE
  14 x 14 inches

NOTE
  Separate the yarn and work all stitches with a
single ply.

INSTRUCTIONS

The design for the pillow has been divided into four quarters. In each section are shown the entire flower and the border pattern for that section plus an overlapping portion of the adjoining border. This is to help align the sections correctly.

Fold a piece of tracing paper into quarters. Open it flat and place the upper right quadrant over the chart for Flower #1 so the border lines at the bottom and on the left edge are about 1/8 inch above the horizontal fold and the same distance from the vertical fold. Trace. Move paper so the upper left quadrant is over Flower #2 and match up small triangles and borders carefully. Trace. Repeat for Flowers 3 and 4 placing #3 under #1, #4 under #2.

Cut an 18-inch square from the linen. Center the design on the square and transfer it.

Flower #1. Outline the center section of the flower with a row of French Knots in 466. Then fill in the entire section with French Knots, working in concentric rows and using the colors in the order listed (492, 496, 015) so the area shades from dark to light. Place the knots close together to cover the linen completely.

Work the Trellis Couching for the petals, using the first number noted for the laid threads and the second for the tie-downs. Outline the petals with the colors noted.

The Split Stitch leaves are to be worked in concentric rows, beginning at the outside edge with the first number listed and following with one row each of the other colors in the order in which they appear.

Flower #2. Outline the large winged petals with a row of Back Stitch in 466. Fill in the petals with solid French Knots, using the colors as in the center section of Flower #1. Outline the areas to be worked in Fishbone with a row of Split Stitch in matching color to add extra depth to the stitches. Slant Satin Stitches and Roumanian Couching in the direction shown by the arrows.

Flower #3. Most stitches are to be worked as in Flowers 1 and 2 (slanting in direction of arrows, shading French Knot center section from dark to light, etc.). Work long leaf in Chain Stitch, beginning with an outline of 492, then working in concentric rows using 496 and 015.

Flower #4. Work cluster of stamen at top of flower in French Knots in the colors noted. The stem of each cluster matches the color of the French Knots. Outline the flower and the scalloped inside edge with Back Stitch in color 466. Then work the French Knot filling, letting the Knots overlap the Back Stitches slightly. Work the Trellis Couching as always, using the first color for the laid threads, the second for the tie-downs. Note that the Buttonhole Stitch border of that section is reversed to create the spiked edge.

Borders. The borders represent a lot of Satin Stitch and could be tiresome if left to be worked all at once. I prefer to do a little at a time as I go. Outline the rows with Split Stitch on each side before working the Satin Stitch. Begin and end all threads on the top and do not cut them off. Leave them and hold them under the Satin Stitch as extra padding. This makes a heavy border that looks like it has cording under it.

Finish all embroidery. Block and construct pillow according to the directions on page 140.

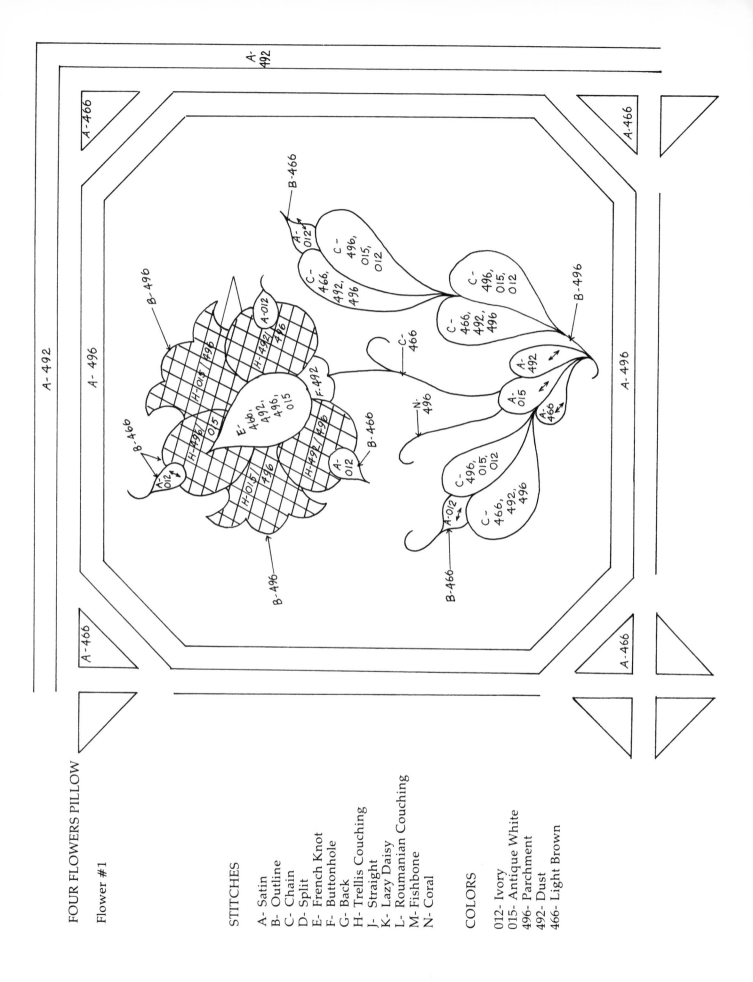

FOUR FLOWERS PILLOW

Flower #1

STITCHES

A- Satin
B- Outline
C- Chain
D- Split
E- French Knot
F- Buttonhole
G- Back
H- Trellis Couching
J- Straight
K- Lazy Daisy
L- Roumanian Couching
M- Fishbone
N- Coral

COLORS

012- Ivory
015- Antique White
496- Parchment
492- Dust
466- Light Brown

96

FOUR FLOWERS PILLOW

Flower #2

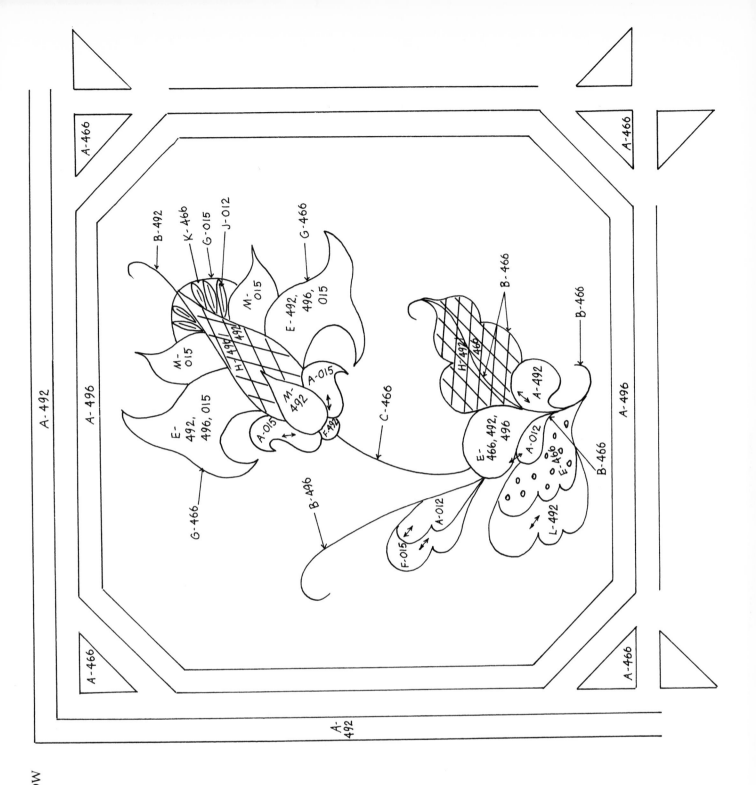

FOUR FLOWERS PILLOW

Flower #3

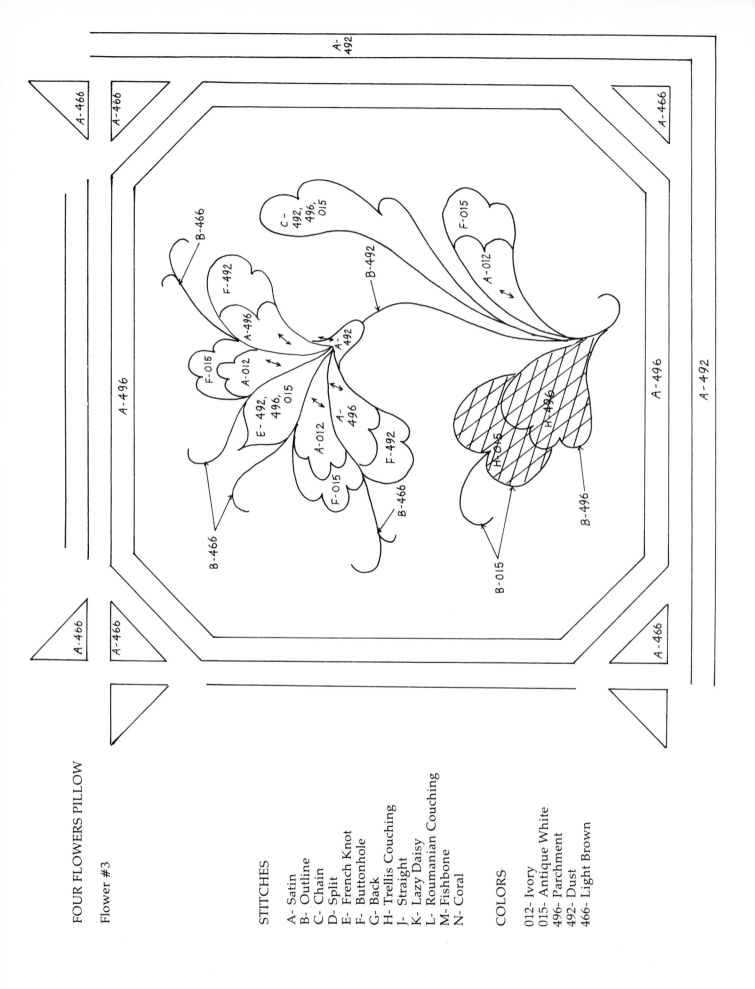

STITCHES

A- Satin
B- Outline
C- Chain
D- Split
E- French Knot
F- Buttonhole
G- Back
H- Trellis Couching
J- Straight
K- Lazy Daisy
L- Roumanian Couching
M- Fishbone
N- Coral

COLORS

012- Ivory
015- Antique White
496- Parchment
492- Dust
466- Light Brown

FOUR FLOWERS PILLOW

Flower #4

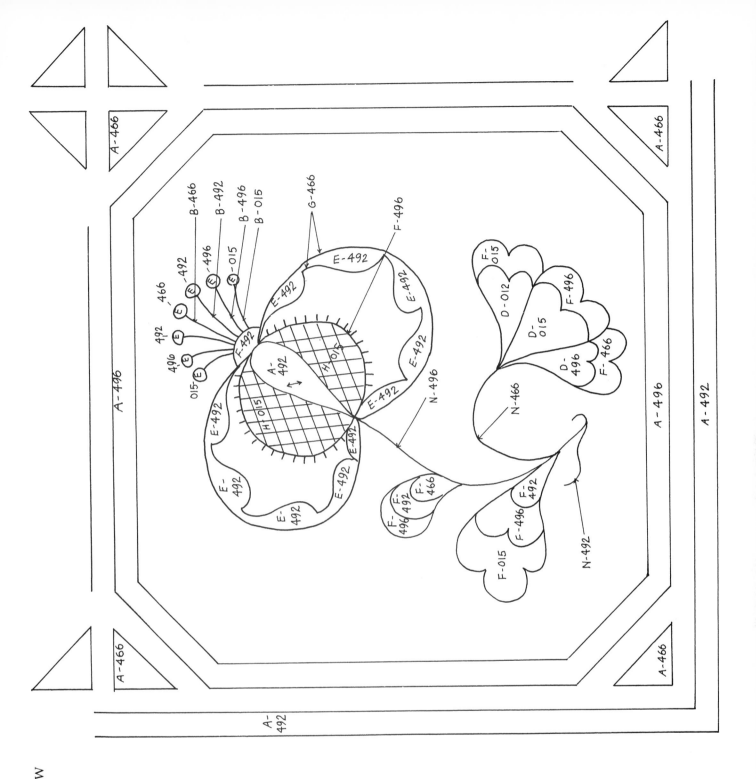

Tulip Eyeglass Case

A simple design, two stitches, and vivid color all combine to make this large eyeglass case a fashion accessory. The tulip is worked on both sides, and the case is piped and lined in bright contrasting linen.

MATERIALS
    Linen, bright orange, 7 x 18 inches
    Linen, dark green 6 x 15 inches
    Interfacing, 3½ x 14 inches
    Crewel yarn: 510, Medium Green, 12 yards;
        452, Light Yellow, 5 yards; 960, Burnt Orange, 7 yards; 958, Dark Orange, 8 yards;
        R-10, True Red, 6 yards

NOTE
    Separate the yarn and work all stitches with a single ply.

INSTRUCTIONS
    Fold tracing paper in half horizontally. Open flat and place over drawing, matching fold line to dotted fold line on the drawing. Trace. Fold the paper in half again on the fold line and trace the tulip through the paper. There are now two tulips joined together at their bases. Trace the stitching lines as a series of small dashes, just heavy enough to be a construction guide. Center the design on the orange linen and transfer it.

    Outline the Satin Stitch areas with Split Stitch before working the Satin Stitch. Slant the Satin Stitches in the direction shown by the arrows on the chart.

    Also pad the outlines of the stems and leaves before working the Roumanian Couching. This adds depth to the stitches. Arrows denote the slant of the Couching Stitches.

Block. Trim the linen, leaving ½ inch beyond the stitching line. Cut the lining to the same size. Sew the interfacing to the wrong side of the embroidered piece. Cut away the excess interfacing in the seam allowance. Make a 15-inch piece of corded piping. (Covering for the cord for this short piece need not be cut on the bias, so there will be enough fabric left from the side of the lining piece for this purpose.) Stitch the piping to one side of the case, beginning at the fold line and stitching around the end to the fold line at the other side. With right sides together, stitch the lining to the case, leaving all of one long side open except for about ½ inch at each end. Trim the seam and the corners. Turn and press. Slip Stitch the long side closed. Fold case in half on the fold line and Slip Stitch closed.

TULIP EYEGLASS CASE

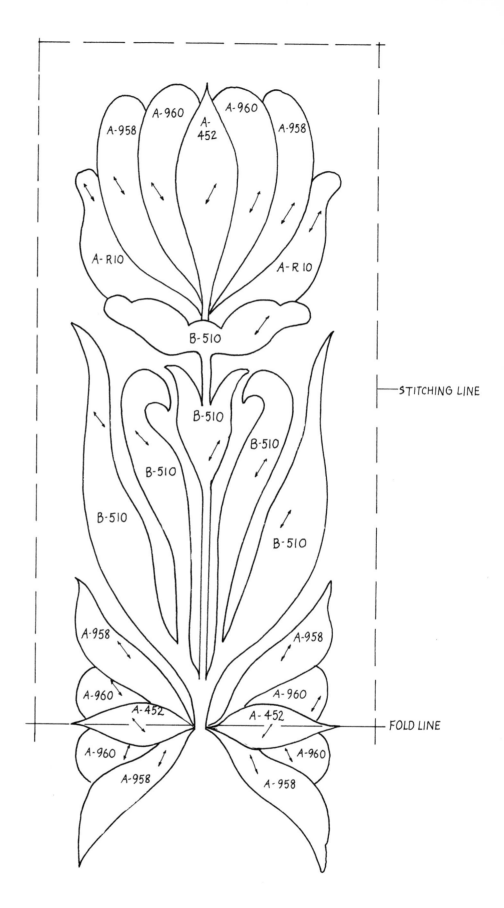

STITCHES

A- Satin
B- Roumanian Couching

COLORS

510- Medium Green
452- Light Yellow
960- Burnt Orange
958- Dark Orange
R10- True Red

Typewriter Cover

Decorate the desk with a practical embroidered typewriter cover, a pleasant change from the standard gray plastic that comes with most machines. Use the plastic cover as a pattern and embroider the linen replacement in the monochromatic pinks shown or coordinate the colors to your office.

MATERIALS

Cream colored linen, ¾ yard

Lining fabric, ¾ yard

Crewel yarn: 26P, Cloud Pink, 5 yards; 837,
Whisper Pink, 5 yards; 831, Pale Pink, 5
yards; 865, Powder Pink, 5 yards; 256,
Snow Petal, 5 yards; 254, Dusty Pink, 12
yards; 281, Antique Pink, 12 yards; 860,
Magnolia, 11 yards; 250, Tea Rose, 5 yards;
234, Toasty Pink, 12 yards; 855, Peony, 10
yards

FINISHED SIZE

Fits standard office-model electric typewriter.

NOTE

Separate the yarn and work all stitches with a
single-ply strand.

INSTRUCTIONS

Using the plastic dust cover as a guide, cut a paper pattern. As drawn, the design for the embroidery should fit on the center panel of the cover for most office-model machines. Cut and make the lining first and check the fit before cutting the linen for the cover.

Trace upper section of design including the dashed line. Move paper to middle section and match up dashed lines and the overlapping portions of design. Trace lower section following the same procedure. Transfer the pattern—minus the dashed lines—to linen, centering it and placing the lower edge about 1 inch above the seam line at front.

Embroider, following the chart for stitch and color placement. In the flower petal borders that are marked "C" (Chain Stitch), with a series of numbers following, begin with a row in the first color at the outside edge and then work succes-

sive rows inside, using the colors in the order they appear. When Trellis Couching is indicated, use the first color for the laid threads, the second for the tie-down thread. When only one color number appears, use this for both laid and tie-down stitches.

For the large oak leaves below each flower, Chain Stitch in two colors as directed. Work the outline with Chain in the first color, then weave the second color in and out as for Interlaced Chain shown in the stitch section.

The holly leaf at the side center of the design should be worked in Outline Stitch in the first color noted, then whipped with the second color as shown in the Whipped Outline Stitch on page 35.

Other stitches are routine. Complete the embroidery, block, and construct the cover to match the plastic one.

TYPEWRITER COVER
Top Section

COLORS

26P- Cloud Pink
837- Whisper Pink
831- Pale Pink
865- Powder Pink
256- Snow Petal
254- Dusty Pink
281- Antique Pink
860- Magnolia
250- Tea Rose
234- Toasty Pink
855- Peony

STITCHES

A- Satin
B- Outline
C- Chain
D- Split
E- French Knot
F- Buttonhole
G- Trellis Couching
H- Seeding
J- Long and Short
K- Roumanian Couching
L- Fishbone
M- Coral

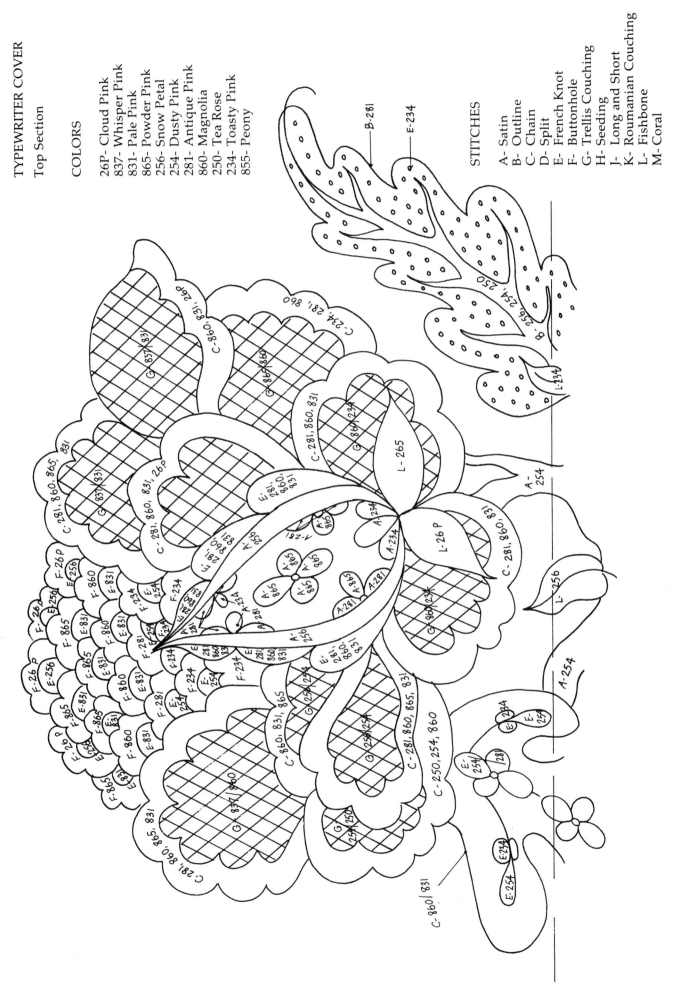

TYPEWRITER COVER
Full View

This reduced version of the pattern shows what your tracing will look like when it's completed.

Drawstring Pouch

The Japanese family crest originated in the eleventh century and was used by high-ranking courtiers on formal costumes worn at the Imperial Court. Early designs included the peony, iris, crane, bellflower, and wisteria. Gradually the symbols began to be used on carriages, banners, flags, and weapons, as well as on clothing. Since each family had its own crest and allowed its retainers to use a variation of the design, there are literally thousands of designs, all simple, lovely, and graphic. The one used on this pouch is a circular arrangement of the graceful clove flower and plant. Worked in white Satin Stitch on a navy background, the design is a classic accent.

MATERIALS
   Navy linen, ½ yard
   Lining fabric, ½ yard
   Crewel Yarn: 005, White, 20 yards; navy to
      match linen (for casing), 3 yards
   Drawstrings: 1½ yards rattail braid, soutache
      cord, or twisted Bishop's cord made from
      navy crewel yarn

FINISHED SIZE
   10½ x 11 inches (before drawstrings are
      pulled)

NOTE
   Separate the yarn and work the embroidery
with a single strand.

INSTRUCTIONS
   Make a tissue pattern for the bag by tracing
the bag outline on the chart and adding ½ inch
beyond the stitching lines for seam allowances.
Mark the stitching lines and the small squares
(■). Placing the marked grain line on the fold of
the fabric, cut two pieces for the bag and two
for the lining.
   Trace and transfer the embroidery design to
the bag fabric, placing it in the position shown
on the drawing. Embroider entire design in
white Satin Stitch. Where the design elements
adjoin, work the individual segments in different directions so they will stand apart from their
neighbors. Add design details at center of
flower petals with a small Straight Stitch in
navy.
   Block the completed embroidery. With right
sides together, stitch the bag sections together.
Turn. Press seam open.
   With right sides together, stitch the lining
seam, leaving an opening between the small
squares (■) at bottom. Press seam open.
   Pin the top of the lining to the top of the bag,
matching seams. Stitch. Trim seam allowance to
¼ inch. Turn through the opening in the lining.
Close the opening with small stitches. Turn the
lining into the bag along the upper seam line
and press the seam flat. Stitch along the stitching line. If you like, trim the top edge with a
row of widely spaced Back Stitch to hold the
fold line in place.
   With two strands of navy crewel yarn, work a
⅜-inch-wide row of Herringbone Stitch to form
a casing for the drawstrings. Cut cording in half
and insert one half through the casing, starting
and finishing at one side. Draw the other cord
through the casing but beginning and ending at
the other side of the bag. Draw cord to gather
top of bag.

DRAWSTRING POUCH

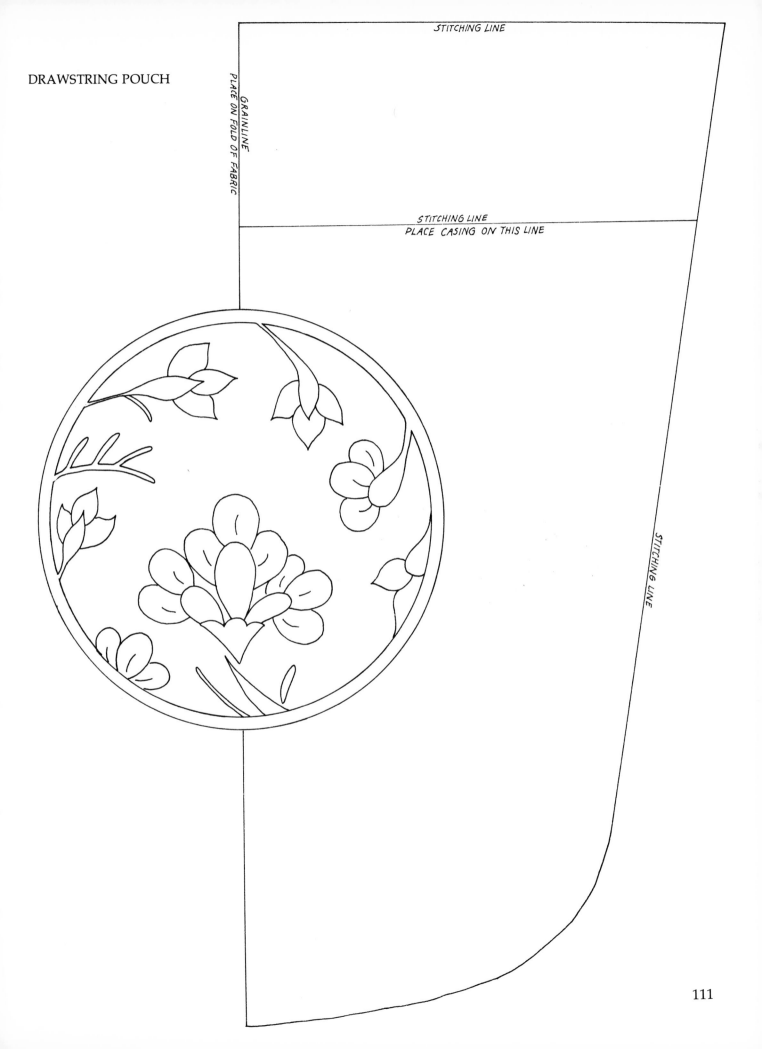

STITCHING LINE

GRAINLINE
PLACE ON FOLD OF FABRIC

STITCHING LINE
PLACE CASING ON THIS LINE

STITCHING LINE

111

Picture Frame

A fabric-covered frame is lovely; this embroidered fabric frame is both lovely and unusual. It features a simple geometric pattern, created with random strokes of a broad-tipped marking pen. The embroidery is Open Herringbone over the stripes, allowing the marker color to show through. Split Stitch then outlines both edges of the stripes and Satin Stitch makes the irregular dots. The effect is an interesting textured fabric that enhances the frame and picture.

MATERIALS
Plain muslin, ½ yard
Crewel yarn in color to match, 25 yards
Broad-tipped waterproof fabric marker
Wood frame, 8 x 10 inches

FINISHED SIZE
8 x 10 inches

NOTE
Separate the yarn and work embroidery with a single ply.

INSTRUCTIONS
Kits containing the component parts of wood frames to be covered with fabric are available and are very easy to use. If you do not get a kit, use an ordinary frame that is 1½ inches to 2 inches wide. If frame is a dark color that will show through the finished fabric, paint it white.

Lay the frame on the fabric and use it as a guide in cutting the fabric. Draw an outline ½ inch larger than the frame both at the inside and outside edges. Cut the fabric at least 3 inches larger than the outlined rectangle. Do not cut out center.

Choose the marker to be used carefully. Those made expressly for use on fabric will not bleed and are available in a workable range of colors. Others made for needlepoint and tubes of color for painted embroidery are also suitable, though it may be wise to test any before using. The marker used on the photographed frame was pink, and the yarn was a matching shade of that color.

The drawing shows the random pattern used for the frame. Don't trace it. Using the marker, make freehand strokes placed like the ones shown. Practice first on a piece of paper and really be free with the marker. Draw the pattern only inside the outlined frame.

Work the Open Herringbone over the stripes in an over-and-under pattern so it looks like it has been woven. Then outline the stripes with a row of Split Stitch on each side. Work the dots in Satin Stitch.

A difference in drawing techniques and variations in the way the Herringbone Stitch is worked may make a difference in the amount of yarn needed.

Block the completed embroidery. If you have used a kit, assemble the frame according to the manufacturer's directions. Otherwise, glue the fabric to the frame, using one of the thick white craft glues. Cover raw edges on the back with paper or muslin lining.

Japanese Ladies

Adapted from an eighteenth century print depicting two Japanese courtesans, this piece maintains the grace and fluid lines of the original but is worked in contemporary colors, while embroidery stitches replace painted detail, particularly patterns in the fabrics.

Colored marking pens made specifically for use on fabric fill the large areas with color, eliminating a great deal of embroidery. Details are embroidered over the color, adding texture and pattern. This combination of pens and embroidery stitches is a useful tool and one you may find other uses for once you have discovered its value.

White fabric, 23 x 18 inches

Marking pens for fabric or ball-point paint tubes for "liquid embroidery" in the following colors: light blue, orange, green, brown, pink, yellow, and gray

Crewel yarn to match the paint or ink colors. Yarn used in model: 783, Medium Teal, 4 yards; 050, Black, 3 yards; 438, Buttercup, 6 yards; 532, Lettuce, 4 yards; 535, Mint Parfait, 4 yards; 537, Iced Mint, 3 yards; 970, Light Orange, 3 yards; 184, Silver Gray, 3 yards; 247, Clove Brown, 2 yards; 850, Berry, 2 yards; R-78, Pink Blush, 2 yards; 452, Light Yellow, 2 yards (If your paint or ink colors do not match these, match them as best as possible and use the quantities listed as a guide to the amount of yarn needed.)

Framing materials

FINISHED SIZE

11¼ x 19 inches (embroidered area only)

NOTE

Work all stitches with a single ply of yarn.

INSTRUCTIONS

Fold a large sheet of tracing paper into quarters. Open flat. Trace Chart #1 on the upper left quadrant, Chart #2 on the upper right section, Chart #3 in the section below #1, and Chart #4 on the lower right quadrant. Match up the overlapping portions of design. Transfer to fabric.

Stretch the fabric in a large roller frame or use stretcher strips large enough to have the entire embroidery surface exposed. With the marking pens or ball-point pens, color the portions of design that have written color notations on them. (Choose the pens for this carefully. Look for pens made specifically for use on fabric; being waterproof is not enough. They must not bleed. Try a test sample on which to learn to apply the ink or paint smoothly. If you elect to use the ball-point paint tubes, apply color sparingly, as a thick layer of paint will be difficult to embroider through.)

All outlines except those on the faces are Split Stitch. All outlines and fabric details—folds, etc.—are in a color matching the ink on the area.

Outline the blue kimono in blue, then scatter Seed Stitch throughout to add texture. Orange obi is to be Trellis Couching in 970, Light Orange. Arrange Sheaf Stitch bundles evenly on brown underskirt section. Shoe soles, feet, and hands are to be Satin Stitch as indicated. This lady's hair is Seeding Stitch, inside the outline of Split Stitch.

Work all outlines and fold lines of green kimono in 532, Lettuce. Fill with evenly spaced Four-Legged Knots in 537, Iced Mint. Outline the two flowers at hemline in Split Stitch in 537 also. Outline black box with Split Stitch; then fill in with long Straight Stitches, using the arrows as a guide for direction of the stitches.

The bamboo fence should be worked in rather loosely spaced Satin Stitches with the stitches extending from top to bottom. Make two of these long stitches brown to outline the rolled section, the balance buttercup. Lay the brown Couching threads across as indicated and tie them down to look like lashings holding the bamboo stakes. Knot details are just little Straight Stitches.

All of the little leaves on the trailing vines at the top of the picture are of Fishbone in the three shades of green. Unless otherwise indicated, the vines themselves are Outline Stitch in 535, Mint Parfait. The arrangement of the shades of green on the vines is random but has been indicated on the full lantern at the back of the lady in the blue kimono. Arrange the colors on the other vines in a manner similar to that used here. Scatter little yellow French Knot flowers among the vines.

Block carefully so as to not disturb the long stitches of the fence. Frame as desired.

JAPANESE LADIES

COLORS

783- Medium Teal
050- Black
438- Buttercup
532- Lettuce
535- Mint Parfait
537- Iced Mint
970- Light Orange
184- Silver Gray
247- Clove Brown
850- Berry
R78- Pink Blush
452- Light Yellow

STITCHES

A- Satin
B- Back
C- Split
D- Straight
E- Seeding
F- Four-Legged Knot
G- Fishbone
H- Outline
J- French Knot
K- Trellis Couching
L- Sheaf
M- Couching

JAPANESE LADIES   Chart #1

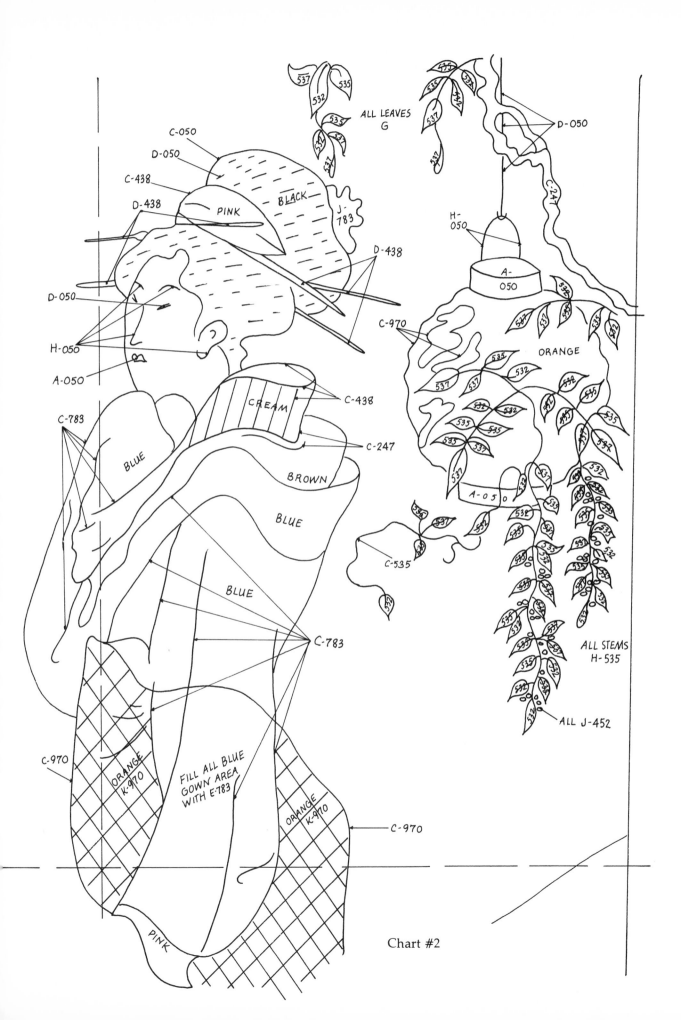

Chart #2

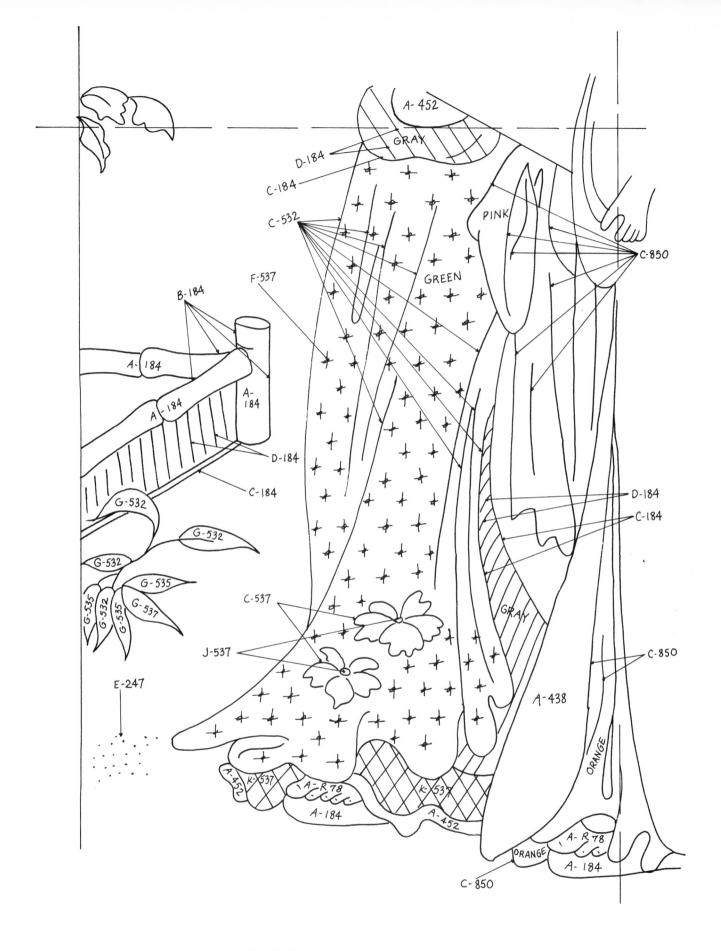

JAPANESE LADIES   Chart #3

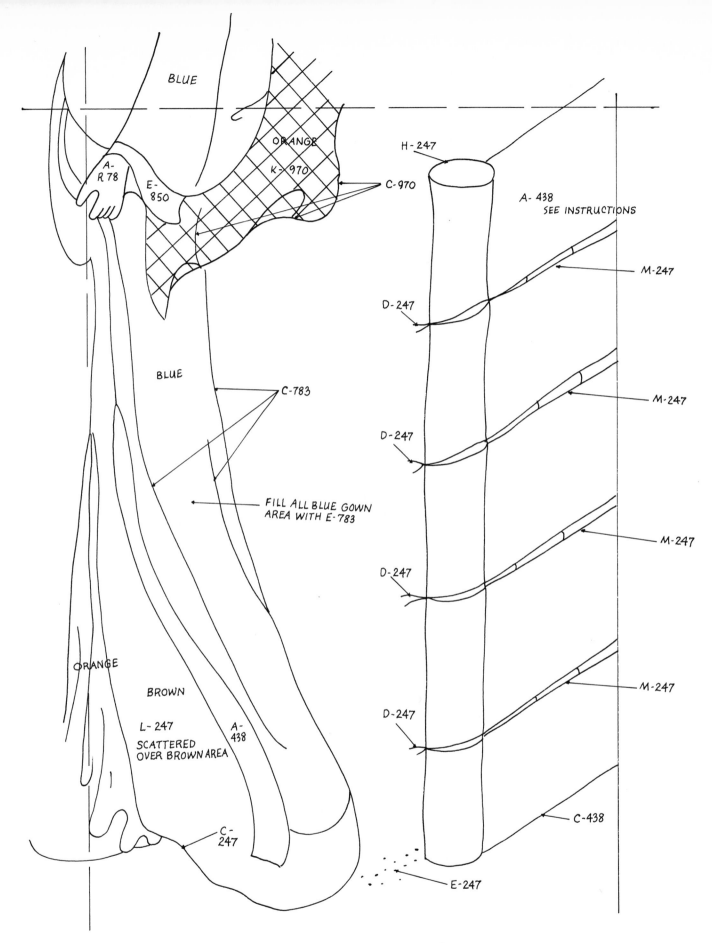

BLUE

ORANGE
K-970

A-
R 78

E-
850

C-970

BLUE

C-783

FILL ALL BLUE GOWN
AREA WITH E-783

ORANGE

BROWN

L-247
SCATTERED
OVER BROWN AREA

A-
438

C-
247

H-247

A-438
SEE INSTRUCTIONS

M-247

D-247

D-247

M-247

D-247

M-247

D-247

M-247

C-438

E-247

Chart #4

Tooth Fairy Pillow

This little pillow makes a charming accessory for a child's room, and the tooth fairy will know exactly where to find the tooth when it's tucked into the tiny pocket. The pocket is also a receptacle for a coin. Trim can be dainty ruffled eyelet, as shown, for a little girl, or the pillow can be finished with a tailored corded piping for a little boy.

MATERIALS

White fabric, ½ yard

Crewel yarn: 758, Light Summer Blue, 12 yards; 247, Clove Brown, 1 yard; R-78, Pink Blush, 3 yards; 437, Buttercream, 3 yards; 385, French Blue, 1 yard; several inches pink for mouth.

Cotton eyelet, if desired, 2 yards of 2 inch wide

Narrow cotton lace, 12 inches

FINISHED SIZE

12 x 12 inches (excluding ruffle)

NOTE

Separate yarn and work all stitches with a single ply.

INSTRUCTIONS

On a sheet of tracing paper, draw an 11-inch square. Draw two lines (one horizontal, one vertical), dividing the square into quarters. Match these lines to the dashed lines on the drawing to center the fairy in the square. Trace fairy, omitting the lettering and flower details on her pouch.

Draw a line 1¼ inch below the top edge of the square and trace My Tooth Fairy Pillow on the line in the position shown in the photograph. Write the child's name in script and center it on a line 1 inch above the square outline at the bottom. Go over entire drawing with transfer pencil and iron it on a 14-inch square of the white fabric.

Trace the little pouch—this time including the lettering and flowers—and transfer it to a 4-inch square of fabric.

Embroider, using the stitches and colors noted on the chart. Work the Long and Short Stitches for hair in lines, following the curves of the curls. Embroider the face in Satin Stitch, then add facial features on top of the stitches.

Work the shadow lines of the gown in Split Stitch in the darker blue, then work the Long and Short, filling the entire area and using the arrows on the chart as a guide to stitch direction. Embroider only the ribbon of the pouch on the pillow top. On the small square of fabric, embroider pocket details. Make the little flowers of a group of five colored French Knots surrounding one yellow French Knot center. Alternate pink and blue flowers as indicated on one side of the drawing. Work the tiny lettering in blue Back Stitch.

Block both pieces. Cut out pocket, leaving ¼ inch beyond outline on all sides. Press raw edges to inside and fasten top hem with small stitches. Sew pocket over outline on pillow top. Gather narrow lace and whip it around edges of pocket.

Measure 1½ inches beyond the square outline and mark cutting line. Trim. Finish pillow, inserting ruffle in seam or omitting it as desired.

TOOTH FAIRY PILLOW

COLORS

758- Light Summer Blue
247- Clove Brown
R78- Pink Blush
437- Buttercream
385- French Blue
Pink for mouth

STITCHES

A- Satin
B- Long and Short
C- Outline
D- French Knot
E- Fly
F- Split
G- Back
H- Straight

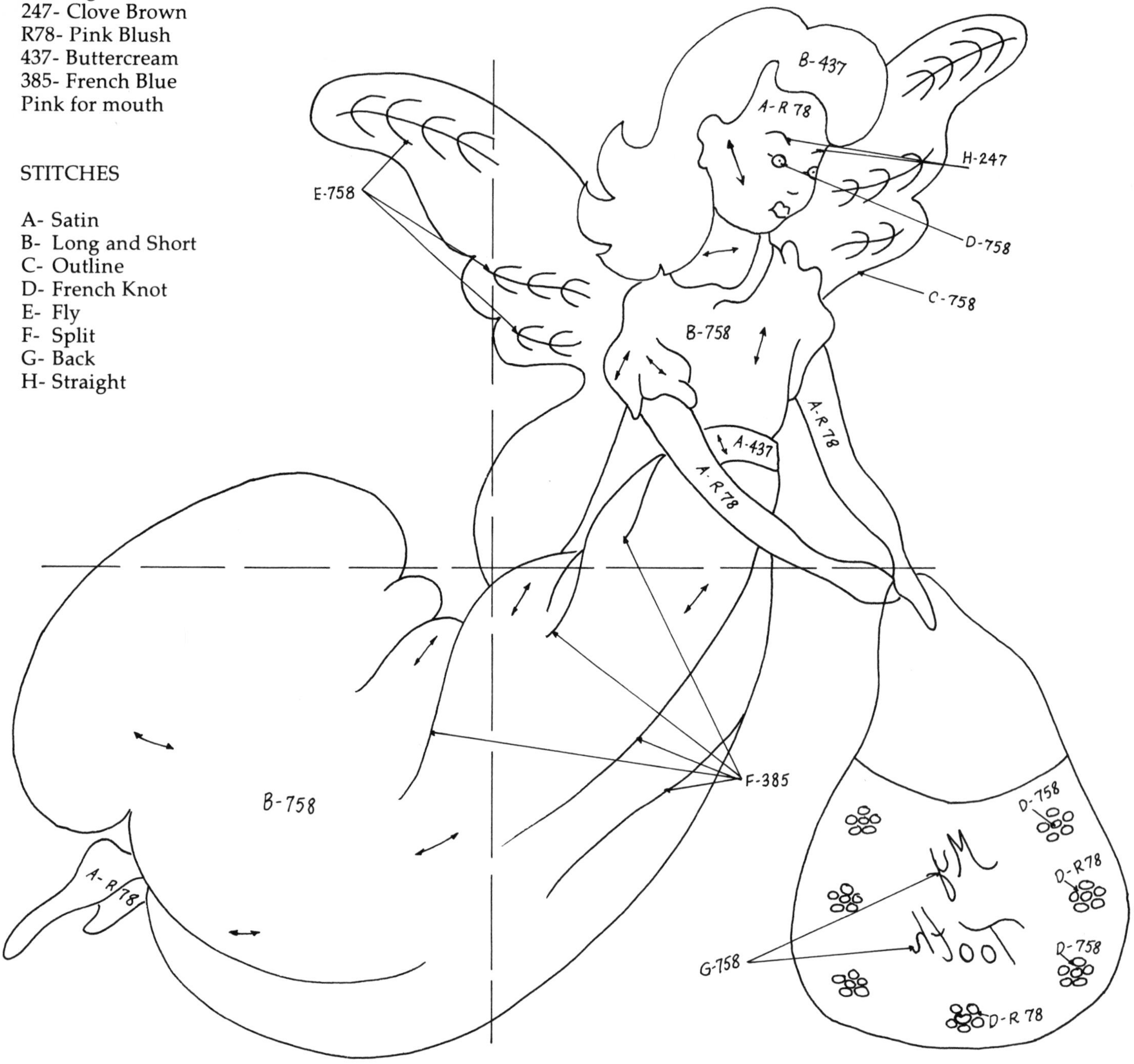

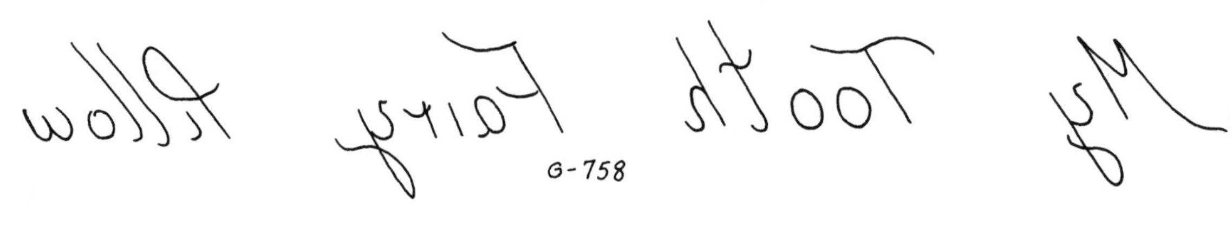

B-437
A-R 78
H-247
D-758
C-758
E-758
B-758
A-R 78
A-437
A-R 78
B-758
A-R 78
F-385
D-758
D-R 78
D-758
D-R 78
G-758
My Tooth
G-758

My Tooth Fairy Pillow

White Wool Afghan

A lovely piece of white wool with a colorful crewel border and generous 4-inch fringe makes a luxurious afghan, a pleasant change from knitted and crocheted throws. The bright pastels of the crewel border show to best advantage on the soft white background.

The border is a repeat—three times for each side of the square—and all repeats have been worked exactly alike. It would also be fun to work each repeat with a different set of stitches and a new arrangement of colors. Use the border for other projects; it would be pretty on a skirt or a narrow bell pull.

125

Square of white wool flannel or other smooth soft fabric, 52 inches

Crewel yarn: 855, Peony, 15 yards; 860, Magnolia Pink, 15 yards; 865, Powder Pink, 14 yards; 831, Pale Pink, 13 yards; 510, Medium Green, 24 yards; 555, Green Giant, 24 yards; 570, Celery Leaf, 12 yards; 575, Spring Pea Green, 7 yards; 452, Light Yellow, 16 yards; 458, Daffodil, 12 yards; 852, Coral, 6 yards; 988, Peach, 6 yards; 385, French Blue, 8 yards; 386, Blue Balloon, 8 yards; 395, Light Blue, 7 yards; 621, Aster, 5 yards; 631, Light Iris, 6 yards

Fringe, about 60 yards pink or another color from the embroidery

FINISHED SIZE
51 x 51 inches

NOTE
Work all stitches with a single strand of yarn.

INSTRUCTIONS

This piece of fabric was 54 inches wide, but by the time the extra wide selvedges were removed and the fabric straightened, a 52-inch square seemed best. Size can vary, but it means that the border will have to be moved in order to fit. For instance, if the fabric is larger, the distance between the hem and the embroidery will have to be larger; the opposite is true with a smaller square.

Cut the fabric square, making certain all edges are perfectly straight. With the sewing machine, run a row of stitching around the square, as close as possible to the edges. Turn back once for a narrow hem and stitch it in place by hand. (Fringe will cover any raw edges, and this makes a nice narrow hem for this purpose.)

The drawing of the design has been divided into two sections. Trace the left section first. Then, using the duplicated portions of design as a guide, line up the right portion and trace it to complete one entire motif. Trace the motif twelve times. Place a basting thread on a straight line 6 inches in from the hem on all four sides of the square. Use the basting line as a guide in placing the border transfers.

Line up the tracings end to end, with the bottom edge of the design on the basting thread, and leave about ½ inch between repeats. Pin all twelve border sections in place, adjusting if necessary. Transfer.

Embroider, following the chart for color and stitch placement. Two flower centers are marked: C–452, 458. This indicates that an outline of 452 should be worked and the rest of the area then filled with 458. Other stitches and instructions are routine.

Complete embroidery. Block or wash as necessary. Cut yarn for fringe into 8-inch lengths. Working from the wrong side with a small steel crochet hook, knot the fringes over the hem. Place fringes close together so the knots completely cover the hem. Trim fringe to even it.

WHITE WOOL AFGHAN (Detail)

This reduced version of the pattern shows what your tracing will look like when it's completed.

WHITE WOOL AFGHAN

STITCHES

A- Satin
B- Outline
C- French Knot
D- Roumanian Couching
E- Split
F- Trellis Couching
G- Fishbone
H- Coral
J- Buttonhole
K- Long and Short
L- Chain
M- Lazy Daisy

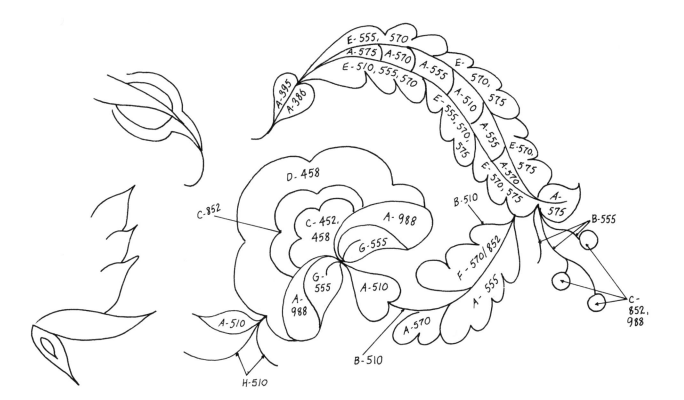

COLORS

855- Peony
860- Magnolia Pink
865- Powder Pink
831- Pale Pink
510- Medium Green
555- Green Giant
570- Celery Leaf
575- Spring Pea Green
452- Light Yellow
458- Daffodil
852- Coral
988- Peach
385- French Blue
386- Blue Balloon
395- Light Blue
621- Aster
631- Light Iris

Peacock Picture

There is definitely a Persian feeling to this stylized design of two peacocks and a fantasy tree. Interesting colors—shades of beige and brown, jade blues and rose, several touches of gold for bright accent—and just eight stitches combine to make a pretty picture of lovely texture and symmetry.

MATERIALS

Cream colored linen, 17 x 15 inches

Crewel yarn: 015, Antique White, 9 yards; 496, Parchment, 5 yards; 492, Dust, 5 yards; 466, Light Brown, 5 yards; 410, Coppertone, 5 yards; 247, Clove Brown, 5 yards; 354, Light Foam, 6 yards; 352, Foam, 6 yards; 367, Sea Green, 4 yards; 340, Jade, 4 yards; 256, Snow Petal, 5 yards; 254, Dusty Pink, 6 yards; 250, Tea Rose, 3 yards; 438, Buttercup, 4 yards; 453, Warm Sands, 4 yards

Framing materials as shown

FINISHED SIZE

Design area is 11 x 13 inches
Frame is 23 x 18¾ inches

NOTE

Separate the yarn and work all embroidery with a single strand.

INSTRUCTIONS

Fold tracing paper into quarters. Open flat and place the upper right quadrant over the drawing for the top section, matching the fold lines to the dashed lines on the drawing. Trace. Move the paper to the chart for the lower section and match lines again. Overlapping design sections should also match. Trace.

Fold the paper in half vertically and trace the design through the paper to complete the other half of the picture. Go over all lines with the transfer pencil and iron the design onto the fabric.

Embroider, following the chart. Note that all leaves on the tree are to be worked in Satin Stitch and all berries are to be clusters of French Knots, both in the colors noted on the chart.

On the peacock's tail, each center oval is to be white Satin Stitch (015) with an outline of Back Stitch in 354, Light Foam. The feathers themselves are all Buttonhole in the colors noted. The body of the bird is all Buttonhole, each fan-shaped feather worked in stitches of graduated lengths to form the rounded shape. Work the area inside the heavier lines in the single color noted.

The legs are rows of Chain Stitch, worked closely to cover the linen, then outlined with small Back Stitches in Jade.

The picture shown in the photograph has been framed with a pale pink mat that complements the pinks in the embroidery. The frame is a simple brown molding bought in a "do-it-yourself" store and cut to size. See page 142 for more framing instructions.

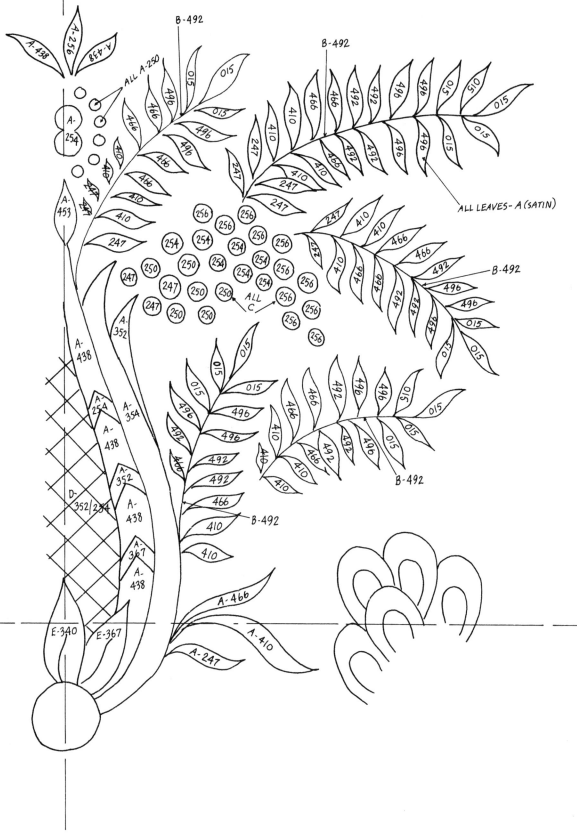

COLORS

015- Antique White
496- Parchment
492- Dust
466- Light Brown
410- Coppertone
247- Clove Brown
354- Light Foam
352- Foam
367- Sea Green
340- Jade
256- Snow Petal
254- Dusty Pink
250- Tea Rose
438- Buttercup
453- Warm Sands

STITCHES

A- Satin
B- Outline
C- French Knot
D- Trellis Couching
E- Fishbone
F- Back
G- Buttonhole
H- Chain

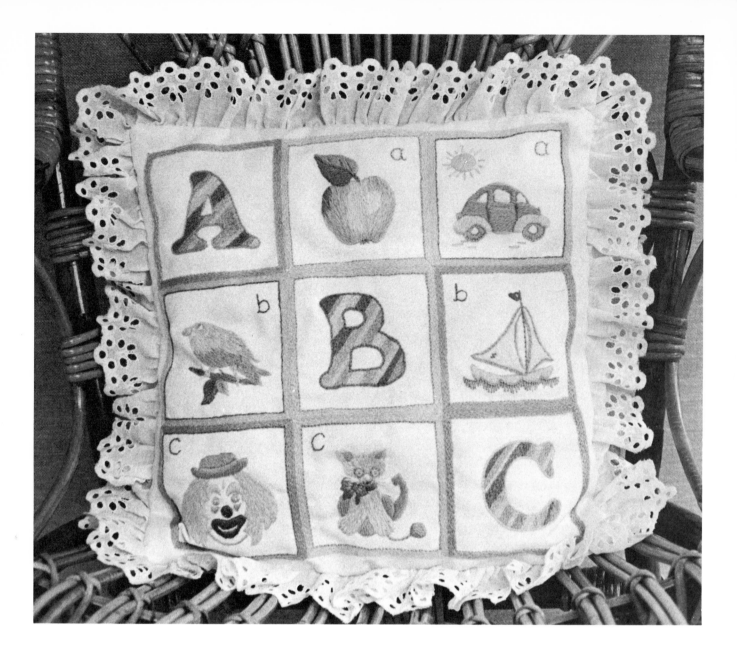

ABC Pillow

Graphic letters worked in a pattern of slanting pastel stripes set the theme for this pretty nursery accessory. The illustrations are simple, much as a child would draw. The letters and the outlines of the squares are Split Stitch; the colors are a selection of bright pastels to please both baby and mother. A white background and gathered eyelet ruffle contrast with the pastel embroidery. This would make a lovely baby or baby shower gift—one that will be treasured for many years.

MATERIALS

White cotton fabric, ½ yard

Cotton eyelet, 2 yards 2 inches wide

Crewel Yarn: 456, Baby Yellow, 11 yards; 837, Whisper Pink, 6 yards; 860, Magnolia, 8 yards; 850, Berry, 3 yards; 395, Light Blue, 5 yards; 386, Blue Balloon, 7 yards; 566, Iced Green, 4 yards; 534, Light Green, 5 yards; 186, Silver Blue, 2 yards; 466, Light Brown, 1 yard; 005, White, 2 yards

FINISHED SIZE

13 x 13 inches (without ruffle)

NOTE

Separate the yarn and work all stitches with a single ply.

INSTRUCTIONS

The design is made up of nine 4-inch squares fit together to form a 12-inch square. Insuring drafting accuracy in drafting the basic layout will be easiest on graph paper. (You can use one of the squares laid out on the charts and draw the layout on plain paper if you are very careful to draw the squares accurately.) Begin by laying out the basic gridwork for the nine squares. Next draw lines to form a smaller square inside, placing the outline ⅜ inch inside the larger square. Place the paper over the charts and trace the design elements, centering them and placing them as shown in the photograph. Go over the outlines with copy pencil and transfer the design to linen.

The ⅜-inch border for each square is to be worked in Split Stitch with the rows placed close together to cover the fabric. Inside that border, a single row of Back Stitch in another color is to be worked. The colors for the A, B, and C blocks are shown on the charts. Those for the balance of the squares are as follows: Apple block, Split Stitch 837, Back Stitch 860; Automobile block, Split Stitch 456, Back Stitch 534; Bird block, Split Stitch 456, Back Stitch 850; Boat block, Split Stitch 860, Back Stitch 566; Clown block, Split Stitch 860, Back Stitch 534; Cat block, Split Stitch 456, Back Stitch 386.

Embroider the letters in rows of closely spaced Split Stitch in the colored stripe pattern; then outline them with Split Stitch in the colors noted. Use the guide lines inside the apple as an aid in shading from the greens to the yellow and white. Change the direction of the stitches as needed to get a rounded effect. Contour the bird and cat bodies and the clown's hair in the same manner. Designs were meant to be coloring-book simple; embroider to maintain the feeling.

Block the completed embroidery and construct the pillow.

456- Baby Yellow
837- Whisper Pink
860- Magnolia
850- Berry
395- Light Blue
386- Blue Balloon
566- Iced Green
534- Light Green
186- Silver Blue
466- Light Brown
005- White

STITCHES

A- Satin
B- Split
C- Back
D- Long and Short
E- Outline
F- Straight
G- Buttonhole
H- Fishbone

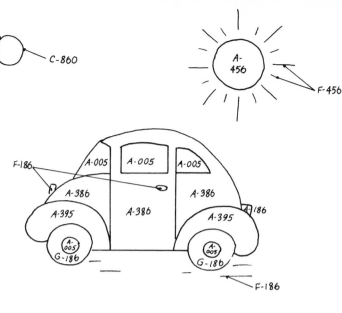

C-860

A-456
F-456

F-186
A-005 A-005 A-005
A-386 A-386
A-386
A-395 A-395
A-005 A-005
G-186 G-186
F-186

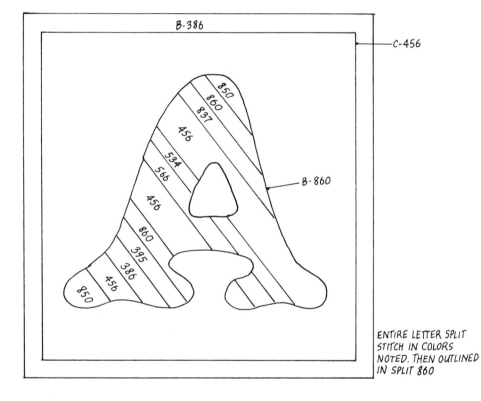

B-386
C-456
850
860
837
456
534
566
456
860
395
386
456
850
B-860

ENTIRE LETTER SPLIT
STITCH IN COLORS
NOTED. THEN OUTLINED
IN SPLIT 860

ABC PILLOW

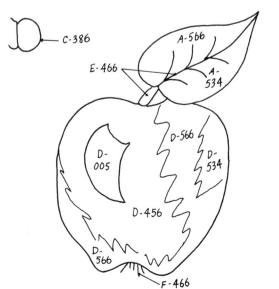

C-386

A-566
E-466
A-534
D-566
D-005
D-534
D-456
D-566
F-466

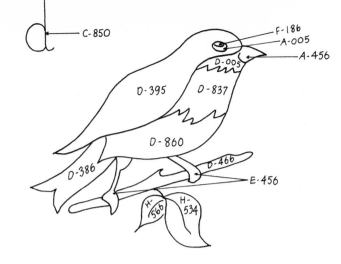

C-850

F-186
A-005
D-005
A-456

D-395   D-837

D-860

D-386   D-466

E-456

H-566   H-534

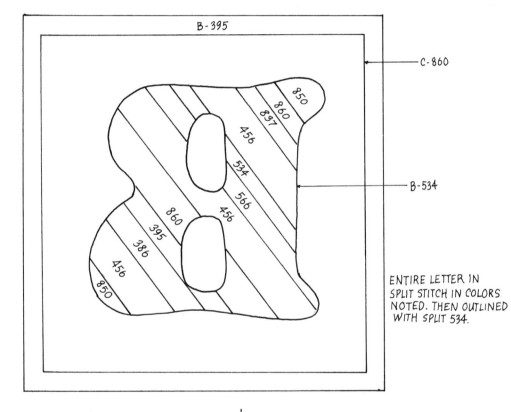

B-395

C-860

850
860
837
456
534
566
456
860
395
386
456
850

B-534

ENTIRE LETTER IN
SPLIT STITCH IN COLORS
NOTED. THEN OUTLINED
WITH SPLIT 534.

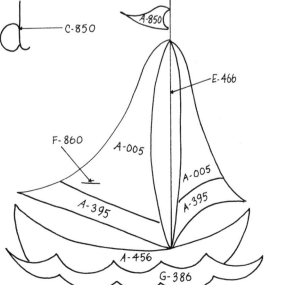

C-850

A-850

E-466

F-860   A-005

A-005

A-395

A-395

A-456

G-386

ABC PILLOW

137

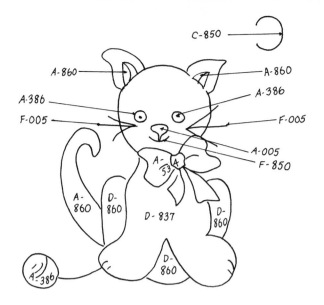

C-850

A-860   A-860
A-386   A-386
F-005   F-005
                               A-005
                               F-850
A-53
A-   D-   D-
860   860   860
       D-837
A-386

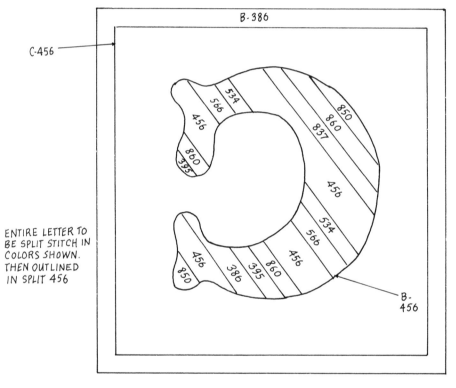

B-386

C-456

534
566
456
860
393

850
860
837

456

534
566
456
850 386 395 860

B-456

ENTIRE LETTER TO
BE SPLIT STITCH IN
COLORS SHOWN.
THEN OUTLINED
IN SPLIT 456

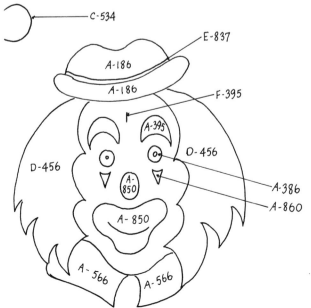

C-534

E-837
A-186
A-186

F-395
A-395
D-456
D-456
A-386
A-860

D-456

A-850

A-850

ABC PILLOW

A-566   A-566

5

FINISHING

Almost as important as the quality of craftsmanship in a piece of embroidery is the degree of professionalism with which it is finished. The finishing process includes blocking, mounting, framing, or sewing construction as required. Each technique exacts high standards of skill and attention to detail, but all are within the limits of reasonably talented persons, willing to work with the care and precision that good needlework deserves.

Of course, all these services are available from professional craftsmen, but since they involve hand labor, they are necessarily expensive if well done. If the embroidery is of heirloom quality or is otherwise notable—perhaps a gift of special significance—professional finishing is probably indicated and certainly worth the price. For the myriad of lesser things that most of us produce by the score, home finishing is usually more practical, economical, and satisfying. There is really an added sense of accomplishment inherent in being able to carry out a

project from the beginning stitch to the final nail in the frame.

Blocking

Even a piece of embroidery that has miraculously been completed while still maintaining its new appearance needs a final steaming or blocking. Soiled or wrinkled pieces need more attention, but even the most disreputable ones usually emerge from the blocking process looking new and fresh.

The equipment necessary for good blocking is not expensive and is often already on hand. The list includes a blocking board, rustproof tacks, T-square, hammer, and steam iron. The best blocking board is an inexpensive new product made from hardboard marked into 1-inch squares which are punctured at the corners. Rustproof nails that come with the board fit into the holes to make for quick and easy straightening of even the most out-of-shape pieces.

The little plastic steaming irons that have recently been introduced for the home sewing market are also very helpful for blocking. They will not scorch fabric or flatten stitches but produce enough steam to dampen fabrics and even out stitches.

If the embroidery is clean, fasten it dry to the blocking board with the right side facing up. Pull the fabric taut and fasten it firmly. Steam thoroughly and allow to dry on the board. (If steam iron or steamer is not available, dampen the fabric evenly with an atomizer or sponge.)

Soiled embroidery should be washed in cold water and mild soap. Agitate gently to remove soil, but do not rub. Do not leave to soak. Rinse thoroughly—as many times as necessary until the water is clear—as soap residue can be very damaging over a period of years. Do not wring, but roll the piece in an absorbent towel and squeeze out excess moisture. Fasten the wet embroidery to the blocking board with the right side up. Pull the fabric taut and use the T-square to make certain it is straight. Allow the piece to dry. This is the best and most practical method of blocking, especially when the embroidery is heavily worked or has large textured stitches.

Although it is generally best to avoid using the iron to block embroidery, an occasional small piece or one that is not heavily embroidered can be successfully blocked with it.

Pad the ironing board with two or three layers of heavy toweling. If the piece is soiled, wash it as described. If it is clean, wet it thoroughly in cold water and roll it in a towel. Iron the wrong side of the embroidery, pulling it into shape. Iron until it is perfectly dry, but use care not to scorch the fabric. Never, never touch the iron to the right side of the embroidery! The padded ironing table will preserve the texture and shape of the stitches, and the piece will look like new.

Construction

PILLOWS

Approach the task of making a pillow with the attitude that the embroidery is an expensive material which should be handled with reasonable care but is not so precious that one should be afraid to finish it. A pillow is a relatively easy sewing project, requiring basic skills and care but no extraordinary ability. If you have never made one, it may be a good idea to purchase an extra half-yard of fabric and make a plain companion pillow before working on the embroidered one. That way you'll gain confidence and expertise—and a complimentary pillow.

The materials needed for making a pillow are: appropriate fabric for the back, cable cord (a soft white cord from the drapery department), polyester fiber filling or a pillow form 1 inch larger than the finished pillow dimensions, and matching thread. Use the zipper foot on the machine for professional-looking results.

Trim the edges of the blocked embroidery ½ inch beyond the stitching line. Using this piece as a pattern, cut the backing to the same dimensions. Cut a length of cable cord 1 inch longer than the total distance around the sides of the trimmed embroidery. Cut a 1¼-inch-wide bias strip as long as the cable cord. Cut on the true bias and piece the strip if necessary. Fold the bias strip in half lengthwise, insert the cable cord into the fold, and stitch as close as possible to the cord to make self-piping for insertion into the seam of the pillow.

With the embroidered piece right side up and beginning at the center of the bottom edge, pin the finished piping along the seam line. Pin the cording with the cut edges along the raw edges of the fabric. Clip the cording at the corners so a sharp right angle turn can be made. Overlap the ends of the piping and lead them toward the raw edges. Machine stitch in place, stitching as close as possible to the cord.

Place the fabric for the back on a flat surface, right side up. Position the embroidery on top with the wrong side up. Pin the layers together. Sew together on the line of stitching holding the piping in place. Leave the bottom partially open to receive filling. Trim the seams and corners. Turn right side out. Fill with loose fiber filling or purchased pillow form. Slip stitch to close opening.

PINCUSHIONS

A sachet or pincushion is only a tiny pillow, and the basic construction is the same. Proceed as in the previous instructions and insert lace, tassels, or other trimmings in the seam as desired. When using wide lace, be careful to pin the lace out of the way so it does not catch in the seam. To use as a sachet, fill with dried flowers instead of fiber filling.

BELL PULLS AND WALL HANGINGS

Successful finishing of a bell pull, wall hanging, or panel depends on precise blocking and cutting. This cannot be overemphasized, for no matter how skillful the construction, the finished piece will be a failure if the embroidered piece and the backing fabric are not perfectly straight. Block carefully; then use just as much care in cutting both the backing and the embroidered piece. Take care to avoid anything that would cause the hanging to be crooked as it hangs on the wall.

The materials used will vary according to the design of the panel. Generally needed are fabric for backing and either bell pull hardware or a dowel arrangement for hanging support. Tassels and self-piping can be used for trim. Appropriate fabrics include velveteen, corduroy, upholstery-weight linen, and the luxurious new synthetic suedes.

These long panels can be finished with a crisp, straight look accomplished with interfacing or may be lined with quilt filler for a softer appearance.

If you choose interfacing, fuse one of the iron-on products to the backing fabric. Base the weight of the interfacing on the amount of stiffening needed. Keep the piece pliable enough to handle and firm enough to hang well without being stiff and hard.

For the padded look, cut the quilt filler to size just to the seam lines. Baste to the wrong side of the panel after the piping has been applied. Finish as in following instructions.

Trim the panel ½ inch beyond the seam lines on all sides. Using this piece as a pattern, cut the backing to the same size. If a self-piping is to be used, make it following the instructions in pillow construction and pin it in place along the seam line. Clip the piping at the corners so a sharp turn can be made. Sew the piping in place, using the zipper foot on the machine and stitching as close as possible to the cord.

Lay the fabric for the back on a flat surface right side up. Place the embroidery on top of the backing fabric with the wrong side up. Pin the two together. Stitch, using the row of machine stitches holding the piping in place as a guide. To avoid wrinkling the embroidery when the piece is turned right side out, stitch only one long side and across the bottom of the piece. Trim the seam allowance and the corner and turn. Pull out the corner to a neat square and press the seam. Turn to the inside and press the remaining edges and hand sew to close. Attach bell pull hardware or dowel arrangements as needed.

EYEGLASS CASES

For the lining of an eyeglass case, choose soft, lint-free fabric that will add a small amount of protection for the glasses as well as a touch of luxury. Velveteen and corduroy are both good choices.

Trim the blocked embroidery, leaving a ½-inch seam allowance on all sides. Using the piece as a pattern, cut the lining. If corded piping is to be used, make it following the instructions in pillow construction on page 140.

With right sides together, fold the lining in half so it corresponds to the shape of the finished case. Sew the bottom and side seams. Trim seam allowances to ⅛ inch but do not turn lining.

With right sides together, sew bottom and side seams of the case. Trim seam allowance to ⅛ inch and trim corners. Turn. Press. Insert lining into case. Use eraser end of pencil to push it in place in the corners. Turn top edge of both case and lining to inside along seam line. Sew together with invisible stitches.

TASSELS

Tassels are a luxurious finishing touch for many embroidery projects. They can be made of one accent color or a combination of colors. The length and thickness can vary to suit any project, but basic construction is the same for all sizes.

Cut a piece of cardboard as wide as the desired length of the tassel. Wind the yarn around the cardboard as many times as necessary to achieve the thickness wanted. If more than one tassel is to be made, count the times the yarn encircles the cardboard so all can be uniform weight.

Cut a length of yarn approximately 12 inches long. Double it and slip it under the yarn on the cardboard. Tie firmly at the top and slip the yarn off the cardboard. Leave the ends of the tie to be used to attach the tassel to the pillow or other project.

Tightly wrap another length of yarn around the tassel about ½ inch below the tie. Knot and pull the ends to the inside to hide them. Trim bottom loops of tassel to a neat straight edge.

To use as trimming on a pillow, pin the tassels in place at the corners of the embroidery at seam line after the piping has been stitched in place. Continue with pillow construction, catching the yarn ends of the ties in the seam.

FRAMING

There is much discussion about proper framing of embroidery and many an effort to establish inflexible rules about the use of glass and mats. Many of these discussions omit the fact that there is more than one correct way to frame a given piece, and they fail to suggest that each piece should be considered in the light of personal preference, as well as artistic value, before any decision is made about framing materials. Styles in embroidery vary so greatly that many finishing techniques are needed to be certain that the correct look is achieved for each piece. While one may need a colored mat and classic frame, another may benefit from a wide ornate frame, and still another may be shown to greatest advantage in an elegant oval. One may look best stretched tightly against a flat surface, while another needs a soft, padded look. The list could go on and on, but the essence is that the choice should be carefully considered and should complement—not overpower—the embroidery.

One of the biggest questions involves the use of glass over embroidery. In most instances, it is best to frame without glass. While glass protects the embroidery from airborne dirt, it also obscures texture and may flatten stitches. Etched glareproof glass slightly darkens colors. Most dust can be brushed easily from the surface of an embroidered picture without damage to the stitches, but in areas where there is extreme pollution, there may be no alternative to the use of glass for protection. Even when glass is used, the embroidery should be removed from the frame and washed every three to five years to prevent rot.

A mat often highlights a picture by accenting a color or simply by adding to the overall size. New mats covered in textures simulating linen, burlap, silk, and grass cloth are unusually attractive with needlework. Plain board mats covered with fabric are elegant, while standard mat board available in art supply stores offers a range of colors to enhance most any color scheme.

Many professional framers will not mat an embroidered picture unless it is going to be covered with glass. This is because few pieces are worked on fabric cut large enough to allow it to be pulled to the back and laced over hardboard. Unless a piece is fastened this way, it will eventually loosen and bubble out around the mat. Assembly at home makes certain that the piece is fastened securely and that this will not happen. Extensions of muslin can be added to pieces that are cut too short to be laced to the hardboard. Use a flat seam that will be under the mat.

Frames in various sizes stocked in variety, lumber, hardware, and art supply stores make it easy to find the right style for a piece that falls into standard size ranges. Frame sections of metal or wood that snap together come in many lengths to solve some problems, while prefinished moldings to be cut and assembled to custom measurement make it possible to frame pieces of any size. Styles run the gamut from simple narrow classics to wide, heavily carved types. New do-it-yourself shops stocked with framing materials and the best of equipment allow the customer to choose and make his own custom frames at a considerable saving but with professional help as needed.

Home assembly is still the most economical and, with a little practice and patience, can be as successful as most expensive custom framing. Measure mats carefully and cut with a utility knife or mat cutter, using a new sharp blade.

Block the embroidery and center it on a heavy chipboard cut to frame size. (If the fabric is thin or the gray color of the board will show through, giving a dingy look, add a sheet of white paper behind the fabric.) Pull the edges of the fabric to the back and lace into place with heavy thread. As noted, if there is not enough fabric to allow it to be pulled back, add extensions of muslin of weight similar to the background fabric, keeping the seams as flat as possible.

Lacing is the best and most permanent method of fastening embroidery in a frame, and it allows for removal later for washing without damage to the fabric. Many glues will eventually discolor or rot fabric and should be avoided if possible.

A soft padded look can be achieved by placing a layer of polyester quilt batting under the embroidery and lacing it in place with a light tension.

Place the stretched embroidery and mat (if one is to be used) in the frame. If possible, back with a cardboard and fasten all into place with small nails or glazier's points. Glue a piece of brown paper to the entire back to seal. The paper should extend almost to the outer edges of the frame and should be glued to the frame only. When the glue has dried, dampen the paper with a sponge, and it will shrink to the taut fit professional framers achieve.

Index of Stitches